Carol Swain has provided in this short work a helpful guide to navigate life in this world with biblically shaped wisdom and righteousness. Building upon the foundation of Scripture and informed by her own powerful experiences, Swain helps position us to live countercultural lives in the world.

— **Dr. Chad Ragsdale**, Academic Dean, Ozark Christian College

As the survivor of a failed abortion, my very existence is countercultural to the predominant cultural narrative of abortion as a choice and a woman's right. I deeply appreciate Dr. Carol Swain's focus on the issue of life in this book.

— **Melissa Ohden**, MSW, author, speaker, founder of The Abortion Survivors Network

Carol Swain is extraordinary. She is unafraid to speak the truth and has been willing to pay a real price for doing so. Dr. Swain's logic is powerful and irrefutable, but her personality and personal stories are what make all she says entirely irresistible. I'm so grateful to her for this deeply wise primer on the Christian response to the vital cultural issues of life, marriage, gender,

materialism, and race and ethnicity. This little book is a big deal.

> — **Eric Metaxas**, #1 *New York Times* best-selling author; host of the nationally syndicated *Eric Metaxas Radio Show*

Dr. Carol Swain is a reasoned and seasoned voice of sanity. She's a thoughtful and pragmatic academic who holds to conservative and traditional views of our culture. In this book she offers a clarion call to a return to the principles of freedom, morality, and transparency that have been the underpinning of our great republic. It's a must read for Americans who believe we've lost our way and need to be bold in speaking out for biblical truth.

> — **Mike Huckabee**, former governor and presidential candidate

Dr. Carol Swain presents the important Christian standards for a successful life through sound historic research and practical guidance—supporting it all solidly in Scriptures. It is a tool for discipleship that will enhance anyone's spiritual life and improve their personal Christian walk.

> — **Steve Feazel**, speaker, best-selling author, and award-winning video producer of documentaries

Unlock the potential of seeing your own life transformed as Dr. Carol M. Swain unlocks the simple answers that will strengthen your faith and reignite fresh passion to pursue God's plan for your life. Her blend of poignant personal life experiences and insightful observations will enable you to resist today's culture that focuses on materialism and greed. As she so beautifully articulates in *Countercultural Living*, God is love and we are to love God and our neighbors as ourselves—all the while faced with a hatred we have never seen before. Dr. Swain encourages us to stop imitating the ideals and opinions of the culture around us, knowing that the Holy Spirit helps us through a total reformation of how we are to think and live in the light of Christ. The scriptural views offered in this book will prepare followers of Jesus to go forth into a culture of darkness and live as ambassadors for our Lord and Savior Jesus Christ!

> — **Germaine Copeland**, author of the best-selling
> *Prayers That Avail Much* series

The authentic Christian life, like the life of its Christ, will always be countercultural. Dr. Swain's contribution to this essential dialogue is clear, concise, and born of a deep respect for the wisdom and authority of Scripture. Some of her conclusions will serve as the final word, a mic drop of truth as it were. Others will serve as the prologue to a deep and nuanced conversation. This whole book will drive you to the Word.

— **Randy Gariss**, Co-Director of the Life and Ministry Preparation Center, Ozark Christian College

Carol Swain's book is the single-most articulate and honest assessment of the problems, challenges, and more importantly, the alternatives to the radical Left's collective positions over the past several years. While addressing race and ethnicity, marriage, human life, and materialism, she offers hard data supplemented with cameos of her fascinating biography. More than anyone else, Carol Swain is uniquely qualified to speak on these topics from both science and experience. Being a black scholar who began life in one of the direst of impoverished conditions and who as a mature adult obtained advanced degrees, professorships, and awards at highly respected universities, she tells it like it was, like it is, and like it can be. Clearly articulating the current crisis in universities and American culture, Swain will awaken any reader looking for the truth.

— **Dr. Mary Poplin**, Professor in the School of Educational Studies at Claremont Graduate University

COUNTER CULTURAL LIVING

WHAT JESUS HAS TO SAY ABOUT LIFE, MARRIAGE, RACE, GENDER, AND MATERIALISM

CAROL M. SWAIN

RENƎW.org

Countercultural Living: What Jesus Has to Say About Life, Marriage, Race, Gender, and Materialism
Copyright © 2021 by Carol M. Swain

Requests for information should be sent via e-mail to Renew. Visit Renew.org for contact information.

ISBN (paperback) 978-1-949921-83-0
ISBN (Mobi) 978-1-949921-84-7
ISBN (ePub) 978-1-949921-85-4

Cover and interior design: Harrington Interactive Media (harringtoninteractive.com)

Printed in the United States of America

To truth seekers and Christ followers around the world. Let us celebrate "him who is able to do immeasurably more than all we ask or imagine, according to his power that is at work within us" (Ephesians 3:20).

CONTENTS

GENERAL
EDITORS' NOTE

There are some difficult teachings in Scripture for disciples of Jesus living in the modern world, especially in our Western secular culture. Our culture has adopted values and beliefs that differ from Scripture in ways sometimes subtle and sometimes blatant. Yet disciples of Jesus commit themselves to the way of Jesus. To be true to his teachings, we need clear guidance and courage.

Carol M. Swain is a strong role model and guide for us in this quest. As you read this book, you will find that she has personal experiences with many of the crucial countercultural challenges she describes in this book. She is an award-winning political scientist and a former tenured professor at Princeton, who left Princeton to become a political science and law professor at Vanderbilt University. She is an author or editor of nine books, one of which—*Black Faces: Black Interests*—has won three national awards. Dr. Swain has appeared on Fox News,

ABC News, CNN, BBC Radio, and NPR, among other outlets. Her opinion pieces have been published in major newspapers, including the *New York Times*, *USA Today*, *CNN Online*, the *Epoch Times*, the *Washington Post*, and the *Wall Street Journal*. She has been a devout Christian since 1999.

This book expounds on the section from the Renew.org Leaders' Faith Statement called "Countercultural Living":

> We believe Jesus' lordship through Scripture will lead us to be a distinct light in the world. We follow the first and second great commandments where love and loyalty to God comes first and love for others comes second. So we prioritize the gospel and one's relationship with God, with a strong commitment to love people in their secondary points of need too. The gospel is God's light for us. It teaches us grace, mercy, and love. It also teaches us God's holiness, justice, and the reality of hell, which led to Jesus' sacrifice of atonement for us. God's light is grace and truth, mercy and righteousness, love and holiness. God's light among us should be reflected in distinctive ways like the following:
>
> 1. We believe that human life begins at conception and ends upon natural death, and that all human

life is priceless in the eyes of God. All humans should be treated as image-bearers of God. For this reason, we stand for the sanctity of life both at its beginning and its end. We oppose elective abortions and euthanasia as immoral and sinful. We understand that there are very rare circumstances that may lead to difficult choices when a mother or child's life is at stake, and we prayerfully surrender and defer to God's wisdom, grace, and mercy in those circumstances.

2. We believe God created marriage as the context for the expression and enjoyment of sexual relations. Jesus defines marriage as a covenant between one man and one woman. We believe that all sexual activity outside the bounds of marriage, including same-sex unions and same-sex marriage, are immoral and must not be condoned by disciples of Jesus.

3. We believe that Jesus invites all races and ethnicities into the kingdom of God. Because humanity has exhibited grave racial injustices throughout history, we believe that everyone, especially disciples, must be proactive in securing justice for people of all races and that racial reconciliation must be a priority for the church.

4. We believe that both men and women were created by God to equally reflect, in gendered ways, the nature and character of God in the world. In marriage, husbands and wives are to submit to one another, yet there are gender specific expressions: husbands model themselves in relationship with their wives after Jesus' sacrificial love for the church, and wives model themselves in relationship with their husbands after the church's willingness to follow Jesus. In the church, men and women serve as partners in the use of their gifts in ministry, while seeking to uphold New Testament norms that teach that the lead teacher/preacher role in the gathered church and the elder/overseer role are for qualified men. The vision of the Bible is an equal partnership of men and women in creation, in marriage, in salvation, in the gifts of the Spirit, and in the ministries of the church but exercised in ways that honor gender as described in the Bible.

5. We believe that we must resist the forces of culture that focus on materialism and greed. The Bible teaches that the love of money is the root of all sorts of evil and that greed is idolatry. Disciples of Jesus should joyfully give liberally and work sacrificially for the poor, the marginalized, and the oppressed.

*See the full Network Faith Statements at the end of this book.

> Support Scriptures:
> Romans 12:3–8; Matthew 22:36–40;
> 1 Corinthians 12:4–7; Ephesians 2:10;
> 4:11–13; 1 Peter 4:10–11; Matthew 20:24–27;
> Philippians 1:1; Acts 20:28; 1 Timothy 2:11–15;
> 3:1–7; Titus 1:5–9; 1 Corinthians 11:2–9;
> 14:33–36; Ephesians 5:21–33; Colossians 3:18–19;
> 1 Corinthians 7:32–35.

The following tips might help you use this book more effectively (and the other books in the *Real Life Theology* series):

1. *Five questions, answers, and Scriptures.* We framed this book around five key questions with five short answers and five notable Scriptures. This format provides clarity, making it easier to commit crucial information to memory. This format also enables the books in the *Real Life Theology* series to support our catechism. Our catechism is a series of fixed questions and answers for instruction in church or home. In all, the series has fifty-two questions, answers, and key Scriptures. This particular book

focuses on the five that are most pertinent to countercultural living.

2. *Personal reflection.* At the end of each chapter are six reflection questions. Each chapter is short and intended for everyday people to read and then process. The questions help you to engage the specific teachings and, if you prefer, to journal your practical reflections.

3. *Discussion questions.* The reflection questions double as discussion-group questions. Even if you do not write down the answers, the questions can be used to stimulate group conversation.

4. *Summary videos.* You can find three to seven-minute video teachings that summarize the book, as well as each chapter, at Renew.org. These short videos can function as standalone teachings. But for groups or group leaders using the book, they can also be used to launch discussion of the reading.

May God use this book to fuel faithful and effective disciple making in your life and church.

For King Jesus,
Bobby Harrington and Daniel McCoy
General Editors, *Real Life Theology* Series

INTRODUCTION

Build houses and settle down; plant gardens
and eat what they produce. Marry and have sons
and daughters; find wives for your sons and
give your daughters in marriage, so that they,
too, may have sons and daughters. Increase in
number there; do not decrease. Also, seek the
peace and prosperity of the city to which I have
carried you into exile. Pray to the LORD for it,
because if it prospers, you, too, will prosper.
— Jeremiah 29:5–7

Sometimes it seems as if we as Christ followers are living in a modern-day version of ancient Babylon. If we follow the teachings of Jesus in societies where everyone does what is right in their own eyes, we find ourselves living outside the mainstream culture. Countercultural living for disciples of Jesus means living our lives in secular societies, where our biblical values and principles are often mocked, disdained, or misunderstood. When our societies change and we find ourselves on the outside looking in, we can find comfort and guidance in the words God gave to the prophet Jeremiah (quoted above). God advised the exiles, through Jeremiah, to participate in the life of their communities and that as the nation prospered, they would prosper too.

Throughout history, God's people have periodically found themselves living in hostile territories among non-believers. Such is the case in the present-day United States of America, as our country follows the trend of much of the globe, including many Western nations. This is new territory for Americans. For more than two centuries an overwhelming majority of American citizens identified themselves as Christians. In recent years, however, the percentage of Christians has slipped and continues to decline.[1] In the coming days, no matter where in the world we were born and raised, our Christian values will be tested and tried. If we are to survive as Christ followers and if we are to engage in the kind of kingdom living that supports our being salt and light to a lost and dying world—we must know what we believe and why.

OUR CHRISTIAN VALUES WILL BE TESTED AND TRIED.

ABOUT MY STORY

I CAME TO KNOW Christ in my mid-forties, after having lived a life that had elements of spirituality but was more consistent with and acceptable to the dominant culture. When I look back at my childhood and teenage interests, I see in myself a spiritual person who knew that something much larger than me was guiding and directing my life. Although I was familiar with Christianity and had some exposure to it in my childhood, I was not raised in a practicing Christian home. My curiosity about all things spiritual took me into many different directions. Eventually, I rejected Christianity and traditional religions for the more acceptable embrace of the "one God, many paths" philosophy, which promotes endless exploration of New Age, Eastern spiritual practice, and other religions. The Christianity I witnessed around me was weak and ineffectual. That's because the Christians I knew lived dreadful lives and engaged in behaviors that were unacceptable, based on what I knew the Bible had to say about lifestyles. As I explored other religions, I came to condemn Christians as hypocrites and to believe that Christianity lacked the power it professed to change people and lives.

After achieving success as a tenured professor at Princeton University, I still struggled with depression and became disillusioned with the world of success. None of my academic achievements satisfied me, nor did the fact I was earning more money than I had ever imagined. Following a spiritual journey in which I was always a sincere traveler, God's providence allowed a series of events to take place in my life. These events culminated in my becoming a devout Christian. After I came to understand the gospel in an intellectual sense, I had a dramatic Paul-on-the-road-to-Damascus encounter. That was followed by a period of growth that culminated with my spiritual embrace of the gospel message and what it meant to follow Christ.

While earlier in my life I had been baptized without having an understanding or appreciation of the life-saving message of the gospel—I had been soaked but not saved—finally, I committed my life fully to Christ. As a result, for the first time in my life I grasped the gospel message and the admonition that Christ gives us to die to self. God removed a crippling shyness that had handicapped me for decades. I understood for the first time that my life did not belong to me. My life now belonged to Christ, and I saw now that everything I had was given to me to help glorify him. My journey has had its ups and downs as I have progressed from a new believer to a more mature one, and my growth in Christ continues today. There was certainly a personal cost to pay for following Christ, but the pleasure and excitement of being a Christ follower has enriched my life in ways I had never imagined possible.

When we are open to the direction of the Holy Spirit and are submitted to godly leadership and direction, we can grow in our ability to practice the first and second greatest commandments with joy: to love God with our whole heart, mind, and soul, and to love our neighbors as we love ourselves. Our ability to practice countercultural living like this originates from the strength we get from studying the Word of God, meditating on Scriptures, spending time in God's presence, and regularly fellowshipping with other believers who can serve as our accountability partners. The community of Jesus is especially important. Hebrews 10:25 encourages us to assemble together with fellow believers. It is also essential that we relate with pastors and elders from whom we can seek advice when the world seeks to blindside us. We are to have confidence in our leaders and submit to their authority because God has charged them with watching out for our souls (Hebrews 13:17). To flourish now and in every age, we must have enough humility to take correction from our leaders even when we respectfully disagree.

AN OVERVIEW OF THE CHAPTERS

IN THIS SHORT BOOK, I grapple with some of the issues facing Christ followers, whose biblically based worldviews place them outside the mainstream culture. This is an ongoing incongruity at the center of countercultural living.

In Chapter 1, I examine how Christians should view human life. Are practices like abortion, euthanasia, or physician-assisted suicide ever acceptable for Christians? The chapter covers murder versus capital punishment, plus the scientific creation and destruction of human-animal embryos.

Chapter 2 raises the question of how we should view marriage. After discussing God's ordination of the first marriage, the chapter covers the factors that play into marriage longevity, biblical grounds for divorce, and contemporary sexuality and same-sex marriage. We learn the difference between marriage viewed as a civil arrangement, with its state and federal laws, and marriage as a holy sacrament ordained by God. I also examine Scriptures that help us understand how we should view gay marriage, especially in places it is legalized and rapidly growing.

Chapter 3 explores how we should view race and ethnicity. Did God create differences that justify "supremacy" thinking and practices among different groups? I discuss slavery in America and how blacks and whites can move beyond the current stalemate toward true healing and reconciliation. I also examine God's view of individuals and nations and what he has to say about slavery and race. In addition, I look at critical race theory, what it is, and how it has impacted the church.

Chapter 4 explores God's creation of males and females, starting with Adam and Eve. I look into the origination of the concept of gender and how different views about gender roles impact the church. We delve into secular debates about the philosophical concepts of complementarianism versus egalitarianism that are part of the theological debates concerning the roles of men and women in the home and church. In addition, I discuss Scriptures that apply to biblical teachings about male and female leadership positions in the church.

Chapter 5 examines materialism and how we as believers should view the pursuit and acquisition of wealth, fame, and fortune. This chapter discusses the pitfalls associated with greed and the love of money. In addition, it addresses the stewardship of wealth and our obligations to support the church and the poor among us, which gets complicated in nations like ours whose governments distribute generous welfare benefits.

I have written this book drawing on my knowledge of Scripture and my life experiences as a believer who came to Christ later in life. As you shall see in these chapters, I have made many mistakes over the years, and given my human imperfections, I am sure to make more. The mistakes I make going forward, however, will be those that come largely because of those parts of human nature that make countercultural living feel challenging but certainly not impossible. My prayer for you is that you will find value in what I have written and that the Holy Spirit will anoint the chapters of this book and the other books in this series so that every reader, such as you, will be strengthened and empowered to walk in the light of Christ. We have an opportunity to shine and glow as we go out as ambassadors for our Lord and Savior.

1

HOW SHOULD WE VIEW HUMAN LIFE?

Answer: We should view human life as sacred because, unlike other beings, humans were created in the image of God.

So God created mankind in his own image,
in the image of God he created them;
male and female he created them.
— Genesis 1:27

Who am I? Where did I come from? And who are these people who make up my family? As a child I grappled with questions like these about life and my place in the world around me. I was born in 1954 and grew up feeling like a misplaced alien in a family of twelve. My situation was complicated by being black and poor in the rural South just when the civil rights movement was hitting new strides. At some point in our lives, most of us have questions about life and our place in the universe. Fortunately for us, the Bible provides answers. We can find meaning and understanding to help us understand our place in the world and the range of life's possibilities in whatever nation in which any one of us happens to be born.

From the moment of their conception to their last breath, every human being possesses a godlikeness that distinguishes us from all of God's other creatures. Our knowledge and understanding of human origins is found in the Old Testament, where God spoke his intentions of creating a unique being that would stand above every other creation.

> Then God said, "Let us make man in our image, after our likeness. And let them have dominion over the fish of the sea and over the birds of the heavens and over the livestock and over all the earth and over every creeping thing that creeps on

the earth." So God created man in his own image, in the image of God he created him; male and female he created them." (Genesis 1:26–27, ESV)

There is a lot of information in these two verses that answers the questions I grew up asking myself. The first detail we notice is the word "us" used to describe God. Many theologians recognize the "us" here as the Godhead of the Trinity: Father, Son, and Holy Spirit. God gave mankind authority and stewardship over the earth and all its inhabitants. We also learn about the biological difference between men and women, which is of growing significance in today's gender-confused world. The world says that gender is fluid and that men can be women and women can be men. But God's Word refers to males and females from the beginning. As we shall see in a later chapter, our biological differences correspond to the unique roles men and women play in life.

This passage also answers the question of where we came from. Human beings did not evolve out of nothingness, nor are we God's afterthought. Each human life has purpose, potential, and meaning. This

EACH HUMAN LIFE HAS PURPOSE, POTENTIAL, AND MEANING.

includes children born with severe birth defects such as Down's syndrome, spina bifida, and anencephaly, as well as adults who suffer from debilitating conditions such as

Alzheimer's disease. We know from John 3:16 the heart of our faith: "For God so loved the world that he gave his one and only Son, that whoever believes in him shall not perish but have eternal life." God is love (1 John 4:7–21). This extends to *all people*, whoever believes. Therefore, he has compassion and love for the physically and mentally impaired.

As Christians, we categorically reject the reasoning of moral philosophers, such as Peter Singer, who argue that parents should be allowed to kill "defective" babies with severe disabilities. Our God values human life at every stage of development. Not even a sparrow falls to the ground without his knowledge (Matthew 10:29). We know from the prophet Isaiah that we are not in the same league as God:

> "For my thoughts are not your thoughts, neither are your ways my ways," declares the Lord. "As the heavens are higher than the earth, so are my ways higher than your ways and my thoughts than your thoughts." (Isaiah 55:8–9)

Not even the great Albert Einstein can boast of the divine wisdom and understanding of the creator God—the God who made a universe that causes all people to ponder the meaning of life and where they fit.

"YOU SHALL NOT MURDER!"

STARTING WITH THE DEATH of Abel, God distinguishes between those who are killed by others and deaths that occur in situations such as wars, accidental deaths, and government-mandated capital punishment. Exodus 20:3–17 lists the Ten Commandments God gave the Israelites. The sixth commandment states, "You shall not murder" (v. 13). Honor killings, abortion, euthanasia, and suicide are forms of murder that God prohibits here because they involve the taking of an innocent life. According to Genesis 4:10, innocent blood cries out from the grave: "The LORD said, 'What have you done? Listen! Your brother's blood cries out to me from the ground.'"

Murder because of jealousy, to preserve family honor, or for any other reason is condemned by God: Proverbs 6:17 tells us that God hates "haughty eyes, a lying tongue, hands that shed innocent blood." In Leviticus 18:21, the Israelites are told, "Do not give any of your children to be sacrificed to Molek, for you must not profane the name of your God. I am the LORD." Likewise, we read in Psalm 106:37–38 (NKJV): "They even sacrificed their sons and their daughters to demons, and shed innocent blood, the blood of their sons and daughters, whom they sacrificed to the idols of Canaan, and the land was polluted with blood." These latter Scriptures should inform our awareness of nations, such as the

United States, where courts and governmental entities have legalized abortion.

There are always consequences for great evil. As we know from the Old Testament, ancient Israel and its surrounding pagan nations suffered the wrath of God because of their detestable actions. As a young woman, I learned the hard way that just because an action is legal does not make it morally right. Like millions of other women around the world, I decided to abort an unplanned baby because of the burden I feared it would impose on my family. I reasoned that if the medical procedure was legal, it must also be moral. I now know governments legalize many actions that are harmful to people as well as condemned in Scripture either directly or indirectly. I suffered some of the many adverse medical and psychological effects discussed in Erika Bachiochi's path-breaking book *The Cost of Choice: Women Evaluate the Impact of Abortion*.[2] Bachiochi's book examines links between abortion and culture, women's health, law, regulation of abortion clinics, and abortion alternatives.

Doctors and medical journals refer to unborn babies as *fetuses*, which can imply by some that they see unborn babies as a lesser form of humanity. This is not biblical. References to *fetuses* rather than *unborn babies* often dehumanize for the world the life growing inside the mother's womb. Pregnant women throughout the Bible are always described as being "with child." Unborn babies are recognized as sons and daughters. Each unborn child has a unique identity and destiny. God told the prophet Jeremiah, "Before I formed you in the womb I knew you, before you were born I set you apart; I appointed you as a prophet to the nations." (Jeremiah 1:5). Similarly, David writes in Psalm 139:13, "For you formed my inward parts; you knitted me together in my mother's womb" (ESV). In the cases of Jesus and John the Baptist, an angel named each child before he was born, giving names connected with some aspect of the child's personality or destiny (Matthew 1:21; Luke 1:13).

In the modern world we continue to use language and concepts to obscure what is taking place. In America, for example, we face the concept of "reproductive rights," which has been disseminated around the world as a positive goal. Yet we know that these "rights" are nothing more than a euphemism for *abortion*. No matter how one attempts to justify their actions, abortion is the violent interruption of a pregnancy that results in the death of the unborn child and an end to the child's destiny and potential in the world. An abortion is nothing to celebrate or shout about with pride, as some women have done in recent years.[3]

Those who choose abortion cannot escape the consequences of their actions. I know this firsthand. Men and women worldwide who have participated in abortion decisions are often racked with guilt, walking around deeply grieved and wounded. Yet Jesus Christ offers hope for people who confess their sins and ask for his forgiveness through his shed blood on the cross. God forgave David of his cold-blooded murder of Uriah, husband to Bathsheba, for example (2 Samuel 11:14–18). That brings enhanced meaning to David's testimony to God's goodness, when he writes, "Blessed is the one whose transgressions are forgiven; whose sins are covered" (Psalm 32:1). Colossians 1:14 reminds us that "we have redemption, the forgiveness of sins." If you are struggling with guilt associated with these issues, then it is important to seek help from mature Christians and spiritual advisers who can walk with you through the process of healing.

There are rare occasions in which doctors recommend an abortion to save the life of the mother. In those special cases, each person needs to seek God's wisdom in the knowledge that he has enough grace and mercy to cover us in every situation we find ourselves. 1 Corinthians 10:13 reminds us, "No temptation has overtaken you except what is common to mankind. And God is faithful; he will not let you be tempted beyond what you can bear. But when you are tempted, he will also provide a way out so that you can endure it."

EUTHANASIA AND PHYSICIAN-ASSISTED SUICIDE

Euthanasia is the deliberate ending of a human life by another person who is attempting to relieve another person's purportedly incurable suffering. It is murder dressed up with a fancy name. Then there is *voluntary* euthanasia (sometimes called physician-assisted suicide), which occurs with the patient's consent. It is tantamount to suicide because it involves the taking of an innocent life. No matter the physical or mental condition of a person's life, every life belongs to God, not to oneself. Job 14:5 states, "A person's days are determined; you have decreed the number of his months and have set limits he cannot exceed." Romans 5:3–5 reminds us how we should respond to suffering: "We also glory in our sufferings, because we know that suffering produces perseverance; perseverance, character; and character, hope. And hope does not put us to shame, because God's love has been poured out into our hearts through the Holy Spirit, who has been given to us."

We have a hope the nonbelieving world lacks. Many of us have witnessed healing miracles for persons diagnosed as terminally ill, which produces its own hope. Plus, we have the comfort of the knowledge of Jesus Christ and

WE HAVE A HOPE THE NONBELIEVING WORLD LACKS.

his finished work on the cross. While the world might view euthanasia and physician-assisted suicide as viable options to end suffering, countercultural Christians who live and die by the dictates of the Word of God believe otherwise. When it comes to suffering, we are told:

> Count it all joy, my brothers, when you meet trials of various kinds, for you know that the testing of your faith produces steadfastness. And let steadfastness have its full effect, that you may be perfect and complete, lacking in nothing. (James 1:2–4, ESV)

Among God's promises is one to end human suffering, as we read in Revelation 21:4–5:

> He will wipe away every tear from their eyes. There will be no more death or mourning or crying or pain, for the old order of things has passed away. He who was seated on the throne said, "I am making everything new."

No evidence in Scripture suggests that God condones or encourages us to take things into our hands when it comes to end-of-life decisions for ourselves or for those placed in our care. This has particular significance for those who care for elderly people and the unborn who are more vulnerable to government policies and healthcare decision-making that sometimes make ending their lives easier than the lives of able-bodied persons.

Modern science and technology are at the point where mankind has moved closer than ever to the rebellious builders of the ancient Tower of Babel. For decades now, scientists have had the ability to clone animals to create direct replicas that carry the exact same DNA as their original. Although there are laws specifically banning the cloning of human beings,[4] it is not clear how long these will stand and whether they have been violated in certain nations. In America, the National Institutes of Health allows experimentation with animal-human fusions that create entities called "chimeras." Chimeras are created by fertilizing non-human eggs (e.g., monkeys, mice, etc.) with human sperm. An article in *Live Science* discusses the ethical and moral dilemmas of creating new life forms: "Human-animal *chimeras* serve as a useful living test environment to help scientists better understand the underpinnings of human biology and the mechanisms of human disease."[5] The ethical issues that make it dangerous and unbiblical have to do with humanity's arrogant attempt to mimic God by creating new creatures imbued with human characteristics. The blending of human and animal DNA is a violation of the sacredness of human life.

It is our being created in the image of God that makes us human and invests us with the unique characteristics that distinguish us from other created beings. As theologian Gary Sutanto writes, "Freedom of the will, self-consciousness, rationality, and the capacity to have religious fellowship with God"[6] are characteristics of being created in the image of God.

As I have matured over the years, found God, and grown in my faith, the questions that troubled me as a child no longer hold sway. Although I don't know all the answers and I have much to learn, I do know Jesus loves me and he loves you.

REFLECTION & DISCUSSION QUESTIONS

1. Read Genesis 1:26–27. How easily can you see the image of God in yourself? Describe what you see.

_____

_____

_____

_____

_____

2. Just because an action is legal does not mean that it is necessarily moral. What is the difference between something being legal and moral?

_____

_____

_____

_____

_____

3. How can grace cover sins such as murder and abortion? Is it difficult for you to extend grace to those who have committed these sins or sins like them?

_____

_____

_____

_____

_____

_____

4. Read James 1:2–4. How would you describe this passage to a new believer?

_____

_____

_____

_____

_____

_____

5. Look at Jeremiah 29:11. How have you seen God's plans to give you a hope and a future play out in your life?

---

6. How can you actively seek to minister to someone who regrets having aborted their child?

2

HOW SHOULD WE VIEW MARRIAGE?

Answer: Marriage is a sacred covenant ordained by God for the permanent union of one man and one woman for purposes of mutual support, companionship, and propagation of humanity.

For this reason a man will leave his father
and mother and be united to his wife,
and the two will become one flesh.
— Matthew 19:5

My aunt and uncle recently celebrated their sixty-seventh wedding anniversary. Over the years, the couple, who were parents to six children, suffered many tragedies, sicknesses, financial hardships, and a brief period of separation. This octogenarian couple is now inseparable. Their marriage is an encouragement to many couples who expect to be together "until death do us part." Other members of my family, including my parents, were not successful with marriage longevity. I believe there's a secret to marital success, so let us explore this from a biblical perspective.

MARRIAGE IN THE BEGINNING

GOD IS THE ORIGINATOR of marriage since he officiated over the first one in human history. The spiritual basis of marriage takes us back to the Garden of Eden, the birthplace of sin and rebellion. The word "genesis" means the beginning or origin of something. In Genesis 1 and 2, we learn about the creation of earth and all its inhabitants. When it comes to the creation of human beings, God had a particular order in mind.

GOD IS THE ORIGINATOR OF MARRIAGE.

God created Adam first and gave him authority and stewardship over the garden. He also gave him an explicit warning with an implied responsibility to share the

God-given responsibility with anyone else who had a need to know. Genesis 2:15–17 states:

> The LORD God took the man and put him in the Garden of Eden to work it and take care of it. And the LORD God commanded the man, "You are free to eat from any tree in the garden; but you must not eat from the tree of the knowledge of good and evil, for when you eat from it you will certainly die."

After giving Adam the warning about the tree, God said, "It is not good for the man to be alone. I will make a helper suitable for him" (Genesis 2:18). God knew that no animal in the garden had the intelligence, rationality, and sensitivities Adam possessed as one created in the image and likeness of God.

According to the creation narrative, God placed Adam into a deep sleep; and while he was unconscious, God performed the first human surgery. It consisted of fashioning one of Adam's ribs into the body of the first woman. Adam was so fascinated by the woman God presented to him that he waxed poetically as he named her: "This is now bone of my bones and flesh of my flesh; she shall be called 'woman,' for she was taken out of man" (Genesis 2:23). The Hebrew writer explains, "That is why a man leaves his father and mother and is united to his wife, and they become one flesh" (Genesis 2:24). Not only did Adam name the animals, he named Eve "woman" after noticing biological and physical differences between them. The woman possessed unique characteristics and attributes that Adam did not have.

We know Adam obediently passed God's instructions to his wife, Eve, who later allowed her curiosity to get the better of her, not to mention her desire to be like God. Love, perhaps, enticed Adam to join her, rather than lose her to "death," whatever he thought that meant when God warned him of this fate (Genesis 2:17). We see how each part of this duo trespassed in 1 Timothy 2:14, where Paul states, "And Adam was not the one deceived; it was the woman who was deceived and became a sinner." Eve sinned and when Adam knowingly transgressed, he became a sinner as well.

Companionship and procreation were important to God's plan for men and women. Ecclesiastes 4:9–12 states:

> Two are better than one, because they have a good return for their labor: If either of them falls down, one can help the other up. But pity anyone who falls and has no one to help them up. Also, if two lie down together, they will keep warm. But how can one keep warm alone? Though one may be overpowered, two can defend themselves. A cord of three strands is not quickly broken.

In the book *Male and Female He Created Them: On Marriage and the Family,* Cardinal Medina Estévez summarizes the Old Testament teachings about God's divine plan for the sexes.

- "that man is an image of God and one of his works;
- that the difference between the sexes is God's work;
- that the reason for this difference is the propagation of the human race and mutual assistance;
- that woman has the same dignity as man;
- that the union between man and woman is so deep that it surpasses even the union between parent and child; and finally
- that before sin there was no sexual disorder."[7]

This understanding about God's plan for the sexes is biblical, even though it is sometimes contested by those who view marriage as merely an affirmation of love without thinking about the original purposes of the unions. God's design included making us drawn to the physical attractiveness of the opposite sex for reasons other than mere sexual gratification.

THE MARRIAGE COVENANT

"HOLY MATRIMONY" IS A description Christians use when describing marriages done by a clergyman or rabbi as opposed to a justice of the peace or some other state official. It signifies the intention of a male and female couple to form a permanent bond in the presence of God and onlookers. It is much like the ceremony surrounding a baptism, where one is baptized publicly before a congregation. Members of Judeo-Christian religions recognize marriage as an institution ordained by God that carries with it certain obligations with regard to sexual monogamy and submission to the headship of the male, who is supposed to be the head of the family and its protector. The apostle Paul writes about male leadership in Ephesians 5:23–24, "For the husband is the head of the wife even as Christ is the head of the church, his body, and is himself its Savior. Now as the church submits to Christ, so also wives should submit in everything to their husbands" (ESV).

In *Mere Christianity*, C. S. Lewis writes:

> The need for some [headship] follows from the idea that marriage is permanent. Of course, as long as the husband and wife are agreed, no question of [headship] should arise. . . . But when there is disagreement, what is to happen? Talk it over, of course; but I am assuming they have done that

and failed to reach agreement. What do they do next? They cannot decide by majority vote, for in a council of two there can be no majority.[8]

Because marriage is intended to be permanent, one individual in the relationship must make final decisions for the relationship to endure.[9]

God expects marriages to take place between individuals who share religious beliefs essential to maintaining their faith and raising any children born into the arrangement. In the New Testament, the apostle Paul warns,

> Do not be yoked together with unbelievers.
> For what do righteousness and wickedness
> have in common? Or what fellowship can light
> have with darkness? What harmony is there
> between Christ and Belial? Or what does a
> believer have in common with an unbeliever?
> (2 Corinthians 6:14–16)

Those who marry nonbelievers in hopes of converting them later are on shaky ground.

CHURCH ATTENDANCE AND STRONG MARRIAGES

BRAD WILCOX, DIRECTOR OF the National Marriage Project at the University of Virginia, and Steven Nock, former professor at the University of Virginia, found that a couple's commitment to marriage and their church attendance are associated with higher levels of female marital happiness. They also report that declines in church attendance and liberalized attitudes about sex and divorce have weakened the supports for marital longevity.[10] Cultures and laws matter. Maggie Gallagher, president of the Institute for Marriage and Public Policy, has argued, "Marriage, like a corporation or private property, is an institution that must be supported by law and culture; if it is to exist at all [it] has to be carved from nature by law, faith, custom, and society."[11] Since the 1960s, we have seen a weakening of the societal supports for marriage in Western nations such as the United States.

In *Soft Patriarchs, New Men: How Christianity Shapes Fathers and Husbands*, Wilcox shows that theologically conservative churches produce men who positively impact their families and societies. These men believe it is better for them as the husband to earn a living and for the wife to take care of the children and the home.[12] These attitudes are reinforced by their church's activities and social networks.[13] The impact of religion and the church is significant among young urban couples who attend church. Wilcox argues that the rate of single-parent households would be even higher if not for urban religious institutions that "depict marriage as a sacred institution that is the best context in which to have sex, raise children, and enjoy divine favor for an intimate relationship."[14]

BIBLICAL GROUNDS FOR DIVORCE

SOME PEOPLE WHO MARRY today and say "I do" are already planning their escape through divorce and elaborate prenuptial agreements. These agreements are meant to minimize the impact of a marriage dissolution. Jesus made his disapproval of divorce clear. In Mark 10:1–9 we read:

> Jesus then left that place and went into the region of Judea and across the Jordan. Again crowds of people came to him, and as was his custom, he taught them. Some Pharisees came and tested him by asking, "Is it lawful for a man to divorce his wife?" "What did Moses command you?" he replied. They said, "Moses permitted a man to write a certificate of divorce and send her away." "It was because your hearts were hard that Moses wrote you this law," Jesus replied. "But at the beginning of creation God 'made them male and female.' For this reason a man will leave his father and mother and be united to his wife, and the two will become one flesh.' So they are no longer two, but one flesh. Therefore what God has joined together, let no one separate."

Here Jesus quoted familiar Jewish Scriptures to his audience, which express God's original intent for marriage to be a sacred union between one man and one woman committed exclusively to each other. But are there exceptions to this?

In Matthew 5:32, Jesus said, "But I say to you that everyone who divorces his wife, except on the ground of sexual immorality, makes her commit adultery, and whoever marries a divorced woman commits adultery" (ESV). The Greek word translated as "sexual immorality" in this passage is *porneia*. Many scholars say that in today's language, the term would include homosexuality, bestiality, pornography, phone sex and cybersex, and other sexual perversions.

In 1 Corinthians 7:10–11, the apostle Paul emphasizes the importance of staying with your spouse if they're unbelieving.

> To the married I give this charge (not I, but the Lord): the wife should not separate from her husband (but if she does, she should remain unmarried or else be reconciled to her husband), and the husband should not divorce his wife. (ESV)

This passage shows that being married to a nonbelieving spouse is not a legitimate reason for a Christian to divorce their spouse. The apostle Paul continues,

> To the rest I say (I, not the Lord) that if any brother has a wife who is an unbeliever, and she consents to live with him, he should not divorce her. If any woman has a husband who is an unbeliever, and he consents to live with her, she should not divorce him. For the unbelieving husband is made holy because of his wife, and the unbelieving wife is made holy because of her husband. Otherwise your children would be unclean, but as it is, they are holy. But if the unbelieving partner separates, let it be so. (1 Corinthians 7:12–15a, ESV)

SAME-SEX MARRIAGE AND CONTEMPORARY SEXUALITY

ALTHOUGH NATIONS LIKE AMERICA recognize same-sex marriages, as do some progressive churches, this recognition and acceptance in Christian churches run counter to the biblical position on homosexuality. Direct Scriptures in the Old Testament give a clue as to God's thinking about same-sex relationships. Leviticus 18:22 states, "You shall not lie with a male as with a woman: it is an abomination." Leviticus 20:13 prescribes death for violating this command, providing a portion of the scriptural basis for rejection of homosexuality.

In the New Testament, Romans 1:24, 26–27 speaks to the issue:

> Therefore God gave them up in the lusts of their hearts to impurity, to the dishonoring of their bodies among themselves. . . . For their women exchanged natural relations for those that are contrary to nature; and the men likewise gave up natural relations with women and were consumed with passion for one another, men committing shameless acts with men and receiving in themselves the due penalty for their error. (ESV)

While Bible-believing Christians cannot affirm same-sex marriages and homosexual behavior, they can show love and compassion for those who find themselves caught up in sexual unions that are not God's best for their lives or the perpetuation of humans.[15]

The world's rules are often arbitrary. Unlike rules in the secular culture, rules governing biblical institutions are not arbitrary. God's view of the family does not change based on circumstances or the whims of a culture. Fornication (sex between unmarried people), adultery (sex with another person's spouse), and homosexual sex (sex between two people of the same sex) are all condemned in the Bible (e.g., 1 Corinthians 7:2; Exodus 20:14). The Bible does not teach that God changes his mind about sin. The Bible teaches that issues of sexual morality are life-and-death sin issues and that our attitudes about sin cannot change regardless of who engages in the behavior. Whether the sinner is a political leader, church leader, or our own son or daughter, we must speak the truth in love to them. Truth does not change based on who is caught up in the transgression.

GOD'S VIEW OF THE FAMILY DOES NOT CHANGE BASED ON THE WHIMS OF A CULTURE.

PERSONAL REFLECTIONS

I STARTED THIS CHAPTER with the discussion of the longevity of my aunt and uncle's marriage. My life story includes two marriages and divorces. The first marriage took place when I was sixteen and I decided to escape from my family of twelve. At the time of my first marriage, I was not pregnant, and I had such a low self-esteem that I was thrilled any man would want to be with me. So I married a man who was four years older than I. We had three children together. Our marriage started without a ceremony. My mother signed the papers and told me I was making a mistake. By the time I was twenty, the marriage had ended and I followed in my mother's footsteps and got a divorce. My mother was a pioneer and a radical. She had divorced my father in the 1950s, which is remarkable for a low-income person with limited education. She divorced twice, just as I would. Neither my mother nor I had a church wedding with family and friends, in which we pledged ourselves to love our husbands until "death do us part." Although many marriages end in divorce, I believe vows made in the presence of friends and family can make a difference in level of commitment and marital longevity.

Although my mother was raised in the church, I was not. My conversion experience came later in life. While I will probably never marry again, now in my sixties, my knowledge of God and his divine plan for each life and for the wife's role in relationship to her husband makes any such decision weightier for me. I know the responsibilities God has placed on the man and on the woman. Longevity of marriage is possible for believers and others who are willing to submit when necessary and work as a team, becoming the one that was envisioned when God brought men and women together for permanent unions.

REFLECTION & DISCUSSION QUESTIONS

1. Taking your cue from the Genesis creation account, what are the major characteristics that differ between humans and animals?

2. List some similarities and differences between men and women that go beyond physical traits. How were you raised to view these differences?

3. What are some reasons for the decline in the Western world of strong marriages?

_____

_____

_____

_____

_____

_____

_____

4. Why do you think the Bible says, "Do not be yoked together with unbelievers" (2 Corinthians 6:14)?

_____

_____

_____

_____

_____

_____

_____

5. Based on the Scriptures you read in this chapter, what are biblical grounds for getting a divorce?

_____

_____

_____

_____

_____

_____

6. What is sacred about marriage? What might be missed when we see marriage as merely a title that is given by a state official?

_____

_____

_____

_____

_____

3

HOW SHOULD WE VIEW RACE AND ETHNICITY?

Answer: God created one human race bearing his divine image from which emerged all the world's ethnicities and nationalities.

From one man he made all the nations, that they should inhabit the whole earth; and he marked out their appointed times in history and the boundaries of their lands.
— Acts 17:26

My views about race and ethnicity are filtered through the lens of having been born and raised in the rural South during the era of legalized segregation, as I mentioned. Everyone's story is different, including the life experiences of many black Americans. I am a descendant of slaves from Virginia, the state where the first Africans landed in 1619 and served as indentured servants until slavery for blacks was made permanent. You might be surprised to know that "permanent slavery became the law in 1662, but any slave who converted to Christianity and was baptized was set free."[16] This type of emancipation by Christian conversion, however, ended in 1667 when the Virginia General Assembly repealed the automatic emancipation for fellow Christians. It was not until January 1, 1863, that slaves again had a chance for emancipation, when President Abraham Lincoln signed the Emancipation Proclamation.

Virginia has been home to prosperous descendants of free blacks whose ancestors learned trades and became wealthy after their indentureship. Then there are others like my family's ancestors, whose slavery and lack of opportunities contributed to generational poverty and hopelessness. One plus for me was having a grandmother who was the daughter of a Methodist pastor, who descended from a line of freed blacks who had served as missionaries in Barbados.

I was not raised in a home of regular churchgoers, yet I understood I was a Christian and that there was a God, although my knowledge of him was limited. Racial disadvantage because of skin color was not a frequent topic in my home. Despite our oppressive poverty, my mother expected us to work hard; she held what I describe as a Protestant work ethic that discouraged the acceptance of handouts. She would later relent on the latter part of that as our family grew to include seven boys and five girls and we needed more help.

CIVIL RIGHTS AND RACISM

ALL I REMEMBER ABOUT race and civil rights at a young age was the injustice side of it. Over the years, though, racial and ethnic barriers gave way in America as opportunities opened for minorities like me. Despite dropping out of school and becoming a teen wife and mother, I eventually made my way to college and graduate school and earned five degrees. I also became a notable university professor, earning tenure at Princeton University and Vanderbilt University, before God put into motion the circumstances that led to my conversion. I now attend a predominantly white church in Nashville after having attended predominantly black and mixed-race churches most of my life. My background of varied worship experiences has given me the necessary foundation and confidence to discuss thorny contemporary church issues most people avoid.

I begin with the definition of "racism." People today are called "racist" and get silenced for reasons that have nothing to do with the traditional understanding of how racism impacts the world. Sociologists Joe and Clairece Feagin define "racism" accurately as:

> An ideology that considers a group's unchangeable physical characteristics to be linked in a direct, causal way to psychological or intellectual characteristics and that, on this basis, distinguishes between superior and inferior racial groups.[17]

Racism is prejudice that occurs when assumptions are made based on a person's membership in a particular racial, ethnic, or social group. Such racism might judge all white people as privileged beneficiaries because of their skin color just as blacks might be regarded as lazy individuals who commit crimes and prefer welfare to work. Such assumptions cause us to treat people differently and unfairly. Within the church and the human heart, racism is a sin problem that can only be addressed and absolved by practicing the teachings of Jesus and understanding what the Bible and gospel say about race.

GOD'S VIEW OF INDIVIDUALS AND NATIONS

THE BIBLE STATES THAT God created one human race imbued with his divine image (Genesis 1:27). Consequently, human distinction of racial superiority based on skin color, physical appearance, or perceived intellectual abilities are inconsistent with his Word and divine nature. From one man, Adam, God created all the nations of the earth, and he chose their national boundaries and their appointed times in history (Acts 17:26). God is intimately involved in the life and birth of every human being. In the Christian religion, we do not get to choose our parents, nationalities, race, ethnicity, or gender. Yet we know that God knows us before we are born. God told the prophet Jeremiah, "Before I formed you in the womb I knew you, before you were born I set you apart; I appointed you as a prophet to the nations" (Jeremiah 1:5). God chose the virgin Mary and her fiancé, Joseph, to become the birth parents of our Lord and Savior, Jesus Christ. Throughout the Bible we see God working in and through the parents of Samuel, John the Baptist, Samson, and others whom he used mightily. God's criteria for kingdom work are not based on demographic information such as race, ethnicity, nationality, or biological gender.

God displays his love for diversity as manifested throughout all creation. One trip to the zoo of any major city reveals the diversity in nature among birds, mammals, fish, reptiles, and other creatures. Why should anyone be surprised that human beings, likewise, share differences in skin color, physical characteristics, cultural traits, and more? Within the Christian church there is a basis for unity that brings together people from different social classes, races, ethnicities, and tribal backgrounds and clans. The love of Christ gives us a secret weapon that should empower us to serve as a light to the rest of the world. Jesus told his disciples: "A new command I give you: Love one another. As I have loved you, so you must love one another. By this everyone will know that you are my disciples, if you love one another" (John 13:34–35).

THE LOVE OF CHRIST GIVES US A SECRET WEAPON.

Loving those who differ from us is preparation for heaven. In Revelation 7:9, the apostle John describes a scene of racial harmony and reconciliation:

> After this I looked, and there before me was a great multitude that no one could count, from every nation, tribe, people and language, standing before the throne and before the Lamb. They were wearing white robes and were holding palm branches in their hands.

The redeemed worship together in diversity as they proclaim the goodness of the Lord.

On earth we have tribulation with every nation of the world suffering from some form of racial, ethnic, or tribal differences that can lead to genocidal behavior. In 1991, historian Arthur Schlesinger, Jr. wrote:

> Within nation-states, nationalism takes the form of ethnicity or tribalism. In country after country across the third world—India, Burma, Sri Lanka, Indonesia, Iraq, Ethiopia, Nigeria, Angola, Trinidad, Guyana—ethnic groups struggle for power and, in desperate cases, for survival. The ethnic upsurge in America, far from being unique, partakes of the global fever. . . . The cult of ethnicity exaggerates differences, intensifies resentments and antagonisms, and drives awful wedges between races and nationalities.[18]

Believers in Christ who understand the kingdom message of Jesus and his call to make disciples from among all the nations of the world should demonstrate racial harmony to a divided world.

God offers salvation to individuals who willingly choose to receive Jesus as Lord and Savior, but he also deals with nations and their leaders. Deuteronomy 32:8 reminds us that when God "gave the nations their inheritance, when he divided all mankind, he set up boundaries for the peoples." He is involved with the rise and fall of leaders, and he judges nations. According to Daniel 2:21, "He changes times and seasons; he deposes kings and raises up others. He gives wisdom to the wise and knowledge to the discerning."

RACE, SLAVERY, AND SCRIPTURE

Slavery has been around since time immemorial, and unfortunately, it is still legal in parts of the world. During biblical times, it took different forms, including situations involving debt, persons captured in war, and indentured servitude, where people were released after serving a fixed number of years. Slavery in the United States was especially incompatible with American ideals as exemplified in the Declaration of Independence's promise that "all men are created equal . . . [and] are endowed by their Creator with certain unalienable Rights."

It was biblical principles that led British politician William Wilberforce to pioneer a successful campaign to abolish the slave trade in Britain. Yet the issue of slavery has divided Christians throughout history because of the Bible's nuances on the subject. It can be frustrating to contemporary Christians that the Bible never comes right out and condemns slavery. In fact, there have been Scriptures that slavery-friendly Christians throughout history have used to condone it. For example, Scriptures detailing curses against the sons of Ham and the Gibeonites have been quoted as a religious justification for keeping slaves in lifetime bondage. Genesis 9:22–27 says that Noah, after a drunken night, cursed the descendants of his son Ham because of an implied sexual transgression committed while he was asleep: "Noah awoke from his wine, and knew what his younger son had done unto him. And he said, Cursed be Canaan [Ham's son]; a servant among servants shall he be unto his brethren" (KJV). [19] A similar passage concerns Joshua's curse of the Gibeonites for tricking the Israelites into sparing their lives:

> Then Joshua called for them, and he spoke to them, saying, "Why have you deceived us, saying, 'We are very far from you,' when you dwell near us? Now therefore, you are cursed, and none of you shall be freed from being slaves—woodcutters and water carriers for the house of my God." (Joshua 9:22–23, NKJV)

Although the Old Testament permitted slavery, it was never a commandment of God. Instead, we find the Bible setting boundaries on how slaves should be treated. For example, Exodus 21: 26–27 states, "When a man strikes the eye of his slave, male or female, and destroys it, he shall let the slave go free because of his eye. If he knocks out the tooth of his slave, male or female, he shall let the slave go free because of his tooth" (ESV).

New Testament passages have been used to justify slavery up through modern times. For example, Colossians 4:1 has been quoted as offering approval for slavery: "Masters, give unto your servants that which is just and equal; knowing that ye also have a Master in heaven" (KJV). Ephesians 6:5 urges servants to be obedient "to your earthly masters."

However, using such passages to justify slavery in the modern world misses some important facts: first, slavery in the ancient world was not based on race (slaves could be of any race). Second, the Bible does not necessarily condone what it describes. It is true that the Old Testament law permitted slavery in keeping with the economic system of the time, but the Old Testament law brought more humane boundaries into an already existing system. For example, Israelite slaves were to be set free after six years (Exodus 21:2) and sent out with plenty of possessions (Deuteronomy 15:13–14). Exodus 21:16 states, "And he that stealeth a man, and selleth him, or if he be found in his hand, he shall surely be put to death" (KJV). Likewise, in the New Testament, we see slavery still as the economic situation for many people.

Clearly, the writers of the New Testament who deal with the issue were not revolutionaries seeking to upend the political order immediately. Yet it is also true that, as the New Testament teachings became disciples' cultural convictions, they would eventually go on to undermine and upend the political order.

Galatians 3:28 states, "There is neither Jew nor Greek, there is neither slave nor free, there is neither male nor female, for you are all one in Christ Jesus" (ESV). The apostle Paul told his fellow believers to receive former slave Onesimus as a brother in Christ:

> Perhaps the reason he was separated from you for a little while was that you might have him back forever—no longer as a slave, but better than a slave, as a dear brother. He is very dear to me but even dearer to you, both as a fellow man and as a brother in the Lord. (Philemon 1:15–16)

The New Testament makes clear that the kingdom of God encompasses people from every race, ethnicity, tribe, and nation of the world. All this to say that in the Bible discrimination based on racial prejudice, wealth, or ethnicity is sin.

In a sharply divided world, we as Christian believers have all the tools we need to model Christlikeness and heal a hurting world being torn asunder by racial and ethnic hatred

WE AS CHRISTIAN BELIEVERS HAVE ALL THE TOOLS WE NEED TO MODEL CHRISTLIKENESS.

and turmoil. Consider the following tools that Jesus gives us to fight racial and ethnic division, which I've included here from an article by Daniel McCoy:

1. He teaches us how to have compassion for those who are hurting: "But a Samaritan, as he traveled, came where the man was; and when he saw him, he took pity on him." (Luke 10:33)
2. He teaches us how to lament: "As he approached Jerusalem and saw the city, he wept over it." (Luke 19:41)
3. He teaches us how to repent: "From that time on Jesus began to preach, 'Repent, for the kingdom of heaven has come near.'" (Matthew 4:17)
4. He teaches us how to reconcile with people whom we have hurt: "First go and be reconciled to them." (Matthew 5:24)
5. He teaches us to seek justice for the oppressed: "He has sent me . . . to set the oppressed free." (Luke 4:18)
6. He teaches us how to bring people together who would naturally hate each other: for example, Jesus brought into his band of twelve both Simon the Zealot (who hated Roman oppression) and Matthew the tax collector (who benefited from Roman oppression).

7. He teaches us how to view each other this side of the cross: "Here there is no Gentile or Jew, circumcised or uncircumcised, barbarian, Scythian, slave or free, but Christ is all, and is in all." (Colossians 3:11)[20]

Unfortunately, many churches that mean well have abandoned the solid meat of the gospel and now find themselves embracing strange doctrines based on secular philosophies such as critical race theory, which is the subject of my final section in this chapter.

PROGRESSIVE CHRISTIANITY'S EMBRACE OF SOCIAL JUSTICE AND CRITICAL RACE THEORY

IT HAS BEEN SAID that a divided church cannot help a divided nation.[21] Churches across the world are dividing increasingly on issues such as race, homosexuality, and gender. Much of the division is being driven by a secular philosophy that has rapidly taken over the institutions of our culture. It's called critical theory. The shorthand description of someone who endorses certain trends in our culture and in progressive churches is calling them "woke." Theologians Neil Shenvi[22] and Gerry McDermott[23] have spoken and written extensively about the incompatibility of critical race theory and Christianity. Shenvi and Pat Sawyer argue:

Modern critical theory views reality through the lens of power. Each individual is seen either as oppressed or as an oppressor, depending on their race, class, gender, sexuality, and a number of other categories. Oppressed groups are subjugated not by physical force or even overt discrimination, but through the exercise of hegemonic power—the ability of dominant groups to impose their norms, values, and expectations on society as a whole, relegating other groups to subordinate positions.[24]

As a worldview, critical theory—along with all of its offshoots like critical race theory (CRT)—is at odds with the biblical message of Jesus Christ's finished work on the cross. Christians believe that human beings are created in God's divine image and that we are all sinners in need of the redeeming power of Jesus' shed blood on the cross. The critical theory worldview speaks of oppressive dominant groups and marginalized minority groups needing liberation. Such deliverance, according to critical theory, can only be granted by the dominant groups, who are expected to divest themselves of their privilege, power, and wealth. In these narratives, ethnic and racial minorities fall into the category of the oppressed. Whites and Western civilization, in particular, fall into the category of oppressors who must continually make amends for societal racism.

It is no wonder traditional churches often find themselves wading into controversies, where they are woefully unprepared for the rhetoric and strategies of social justice warriors steeped in philosophies such as CRT that emerged from cultural Marxism. Books like Robin De Angelo's *White Fragility*[25] have found their way into churches, and a new generation of racially sensitive leaders have begun to embrace ideas that take them away from the gospel of Jesus Christ and toward this new approach. It's a works-based approach too because supposed oppressors must repeatedly denounce their own racism (and the racism of long-dead ancestors deemed guilty of oppression) regardless of whether the accused was a descendant of abolitionists or someone who recently immigrated to the United States. CRT identifies white people as oppressors based on their skin color.

Within the church even, some people make other church members into oppressors or marginalized victims based on skin color, which are race-based and ethnic-based divisions. Whites are deemed as privileged oppressors of marginalized people; blacks are often deemed oppressed. Whites are expected to confess their racism and become explicitly anti-racist by confronting forms of injustice or anything that could be interpreted as such.

As McDermott and others point out, CRT redefines the Christian gospel, the meaning and pursuit of truth, the moral life, and the meaning of sin.[26] It is clearly incompatible with Christianity, and church leaders and laymen must acquaint themselves with this philosophy if they are to be able to disciple and make cogent arguments for truth in our times.

Some have noted how CRT and its relativism enter the church on the coattails of progressive Christianity, which can be seen as a rewriting of the script of Christianity to fit Western cultural values.[27] We must understand the subtle ways that dangerous ideas like CRT enter and take root in the church. Alisa Childers's eye-opening autobiographical account of her journey into and through progressive Christianity describes the slippery slope that led her from traditional Christianity along a path that almost destroyed her faith. She ended up finding hope and renewal through the core doctrinal teachings of Christianity.[28] If we are to be salt and light in the world, it is essential that we equip ourselves so we are not easily swayed by clever manipulations that often play on our heartstrings.

REFLECTION & DISCUSSION QUESTIONS

1. How have you seen racism play out in your personal or professional life? Have you ever had an experience as a victim of racism as defined in this chapter?

_____

_____

_____

_____

_____

_____

2. How does the beautiful diversity in God's creation apply to the issue of racial/ethnic differences?

_____

_____

_____

_____

_____

_____

3. How would you explain the biblical passages that allow for slavery to someone who already tends to be skeptical of the Bible?

_____

_____

_____

_____

_____

_____

4. In your own words, describe some of the tools that Jesus gives us to fight racial and ethnic division.

_____

_____

_____

_____

_____

_____

_____

5. Describe critical theory and the impact it could have (or has had) on you and your church.

_____

_____

_____

_____

_____

_____

_____

6. What are the limitations of trying to bring about racial healing without the biblical truth that we are all made in God's image?

_____

_____

_____

_____

_____

_____

4

HOW SHOULD WE VIEW MALE AND FEMALE ROLES?

Answer: God created males and females to have complementary physical bodies and strengths, equal spiritual gifts and worth, and he placed them in relationships where partnerships and mutual respect contribute to human flourishing.

Husbands, love your wives, just as Christ loved
the church and gave himself up for her.
— Ephesians 5:25

My entry into the church world naturally came later in life with my conversion. This happened after I was a university professor at secular elite institutions for almost thirty years. Within those academic structures, my views of male-female relationships were influenced by the women's liberation movement, which burst onto the scene during my childhood. By the time I entered college in the late 1970s, feminist theory and critical gender theories were dominant. We were encouraged to confront the patriarchal system by which fathers, brothers, and husbands held women in bondage through stereotypes and cultural traditions. Despite my exposure to these ideas, I never became a radical feminist, although I did notice that men held the most powerful positions in society and that some used their positions to abuse women.

Coming into the church and reading Bible stories such as the cowardice expressed by Abraham in his failure to protect his wife, Sarah—twice—were difficult to process. Women in the Bible clearly had fewer rights and protections than men. What is heartening, however, is the New Testament's treatment of women as well as God's fairness in the Old Testament, where he allowed the daughters of Zelophehad, for example, to inherit a portion of their father's estate (Numbers 27:7). It is good, too, that although the Israelites of the Old Testament lived under the stringent laws of the Old Testament, New

Testament grace entered the world through Jesus Christ's sacrificial death on the cross.

Jesus Christ modeled love and caring for women at a time when they had a lower status than men.

- Jesus healed the woman with the issue of blood (Luke 8:43–48).
- Jesus chatted with the Samaritan woman (John 4:1–42).
- Jesus saved the life of the woman caught in adultery (John 8: 3–11).
- Jesus allowed women to be among his disciples (Luke 8:1–3).
- Women were the first to see Jesus after his resurrection (John 20:18).

Then, we know that God lovingly selected Joseph to be the father of Jesus, a decent man who respected his fiancée even though he did not initially understand the circumstances of her pregnancy (Matthew 1:18–25).

As we examine the modern-day roles of women in the church and home, we must keep in mind how God has repeatedly shown care and compassion for women and their more vulnerable positioning in society dating as far back as the Old Testament story of Hagar (Genesis 21:14–20). In recent years, there has been a revolution in the church sparked, in part, by the emergence of the MeToo movement.[29] In turn, that has spawned what many call a "ChurchToo" movement of "woke" women who are accusing pastors and ministerial staff of decades-long sexual and mental abuses that parallel what is happening in secular society.

The mostly male leaders in many evangelical churches face a changing environment that requires the exercise of extreme prudence when it comes to meeting with members of the opposite sex and those struggling with same-sex attractions. Now, every church needs clear lines of authority, accountability, and safe systems through which women and men can seek help before situations explode. And the inclusion of female ministers in churches can be helpful in situations where male elders and lead minister/pastors are the governing authorities, as required by Scripture (expounded on later in this chapter). We in the church world live and operate as a microcosm of the larger secular world, so I will begin by defining secular concepts that have entered theological discussions about relationships between males and females. Then, I will turn to Scripture for direction and answers about how to govern our lives in accordance with the Word of God.

GENDER AND THE CHURCH

PEOPLE OFTEN USE BIOLOGICAL sex and gender as if the concepts are interchangeable. Those who want to discuss the appropriate roles for males and females in family relationships and in the church refer to "gender roles." Yet gender as defined in our culture is not a biblical concept. Male and female biological sexes are biblical, but the concept of male and female "gender" is not. Let me explain.

GENDER AS DEFINED IN OUR CULTURE IS NOT A BIBLICAL CONCEPT.

The phrase "gender roles" was first coined in 1955 by John Money, a New Zealand psychologist and sexologist who also developed the concepts of sexual identity and sexual orientation.[30] According to Money, gender roles refer to what a person does to "disclose himself or herself as having the status of boy or man, girl or woman." "Gender" has been expanded to include non-binary and third-binary genders.[31] Third-binary genders—where individuals reject male and female classifications—are now legally recognized in many nations and a growing number of US states. The concept of gender allows unlimited possibilities that go beyond male and female self-identifications.

This concept of gender was developed as a social construct to accommodate a range of behaviors that conflict with what is considered traditional male and female attributes.[32] A biblical view drives no wedge between gender and sexuality and ties sexuality to God's created order.[33] However, some in the church world have welcomed and now promote secular concepts of gender through critical gender studies, state and federal laws, and misguided efforts to be more inclusive by using the language and reasoning of the secular world. The church, I believe, should stick to the biblical understanding of males and females.

We recognize that God created two sexes and because of sin and cultural factors there exist people who suffer from gender dysphoria, believing that they were born into the wrong body, or same-sex attraction, which is actively encouraged by our society. If church leaders are unclear about their terminology, real problems can occur when legally recognized new forms of gender create situations that conflict with biblical teachings concerning the roles of men and women in church leadership positions. Transgenderism and legal protections for people who identify differently from their biological sex create new and difficult situations for Bible-believing churches. Each church leader needs to be prepared to take a stance and suffer whatever consequences might come.

Problems arise when Bible-believing churches begin to accept secular arguments that people can be born into the wrong bodies or that same-sex sexuality is separate from sin. Scripture calls us to affirm God's biological design, as we are made to be male or female (Genesis 1:26–28). We uphold God's design, while acknowledging the pain and struggles that some experience upholding these standards today (Deuteronomy 22:5).[34] We strive for obedience to

Jesus, and we help each other carry our cross of obedience. We believe God's ways are ultimately best for human flourishing, even when the road is hard for some.

COMPLEMENTARIANISM VS. EGALITARIANISM

ADDITIONAL SECULAR CONCEPTS, SUCH as gender, have entered theological circles and become the latest buzzwords, and this includes the debate over complementarianism versus egalitarianism. These philosophical theories provide a more sophisticated language for debates about the roles of women in the family and in the church. *Theopedia* defines "complementarianism" as a theological view that men and women "are created equal in their being and personhood, (and) they are created to complement each other via different roles and responsibilities as manifested in marriage, family life, religious leadership, and elsewhere."[35] Author Alyssa Roat explains that men and women "complement" each other "like complementary colors work well together to create beauty, or one aspect of a dish complements another."[36] Therefore, masculinity and femininity are God-created attributes corresponding to the different roles men and women have in life. This makes possible the unity and oneness that occurs when the two become one in the marriage union.

The Renew.org Network upholds complementarianism because it is taught in Scriptures such as 1 Corinthians 11:3–16, 1 Corinthians 14:33–36, and 1 Timothy 2:11–3:16. These passages show us that the starting place for this discussion is the creation account of Genesis 1–2, especially the created order God intends.[37] We believe these passages offer God's normative and transcultural guidance for distinctive roles for godly male leaders in the church and respectful and strong wives.[38] Male leaders in the church have two roles: the authoritative teaching role (lead minister/pastor) and the elders of a church (the words "elder" and "pastor" are synonyms). The contrary view of complementarianism is egalitarianism, which is the theological view that there are no gender-based limitations on the roles that males and females can perform in the home, the church, and society. According to this view, Jesus and New Testament principles of equality erased all gender-specific distinctions. The Scripture most frequently cited by secularists to support this view is Galatians 3:28: "There is neither Jew nor Gentile, neither slave nor free, nor is there male and female, for you are all one in Christ Jesus."

In the church, men and women serve as partners in the use of their gifts in ministry. The vision of the Bible is an equal partnership of men and women in creation, in marriage, in salvation, in the gifts of the Spirit, and in the ministries of the church but exercised in ways that honor the biological sexes as described in the Bible.

In the Bible we see women serving as deacons, co-laborers, and in all other aspects of the ministry of the church besides the two roles outlined above. This would include women in positions leading teams, serving as chairs of committees, etcetera, because of their specialized knowledge and professional and spiritual experience and expertise. There are also roles men cannot have in the church and family life, such as leading women's ministry and nursing babies. God's view is equal value, different roles.

Yet the male headship role in the gathered church reflects God's created order. And this role is to be filled by qualified men only.[39] The headship role also reflects God's created order in the home as well. We find the scriptural basis for men only to fill the teaching-authority role and elder/pastor role in the New Testament.

- *On church-wide teaching and authority,*
  1 Timothy 2:12–14 states, "I do not permit a woman to teach or to assume authority over a man; she must be quiet. For Adam was formed first, then Eve. And Adam was not the one deceived; it was the woman who was deceived and became a sinner."

- *On the elder/pastor role*, Titus 1:6–9 teaches us to appoint qualified men: "An elder must be blameless, faithful to his wife, a man whose children believe and are not open to the charge of being wild and disobedient. Since an overseer manages God's household, he must be blameless—not overbearing, not quick-tempered, not given to drunkenness, not violent, not pursuing dishonest gain. Rather, he must be hospitable, one who loves what is good, who is self-controlled, upright, holy, and disciplined. He must hold firmly to the trustworthy message as it has been taught so that he can encourage others by sound doctrine and refute those who oppose it" (see also 1 Timothy 3:1–6).

Now, it's worth noting that Scripture doesn't just limit roles based on biological sex but also various other qualifications. These other qualifications make for what is indeed a high standard for leadership, often waived by churches seeking to fill elder and pastor positions with men who fall short on one or more of these criteria. But God wants us to uphold his standards because his standards are best for our flourishing.

GOD'S STANDARDS ARE BEST FOR OUR FLOURISHING.

The Bible makes it clear that husbands should be submitted to Christ and wives to the headship of their husbands. This basic principle is found in 1 Corinthians 11:3, which states, "But I want you to understand that the head of every man is Christ, the head of a wife is her husband, and the head of Christ is God" (ESV). Husbands and men in headship positions in the church are expected to be a covering over their wives and the members of the church as Christ is the covering over the church. Men are not to be overbearing or abusive to their wives or to the people in their churches—physically or verbally or in any other way. Husbands and these church leaders are admonished to love those they guide "as Christ loved the church and gave himself up for her" (Ephesians 5:25; see also Ephesians 5:33 and Matthew 20:25–28). Marriages and church relationships thrive when husbands and wives and church leaders and members commit to mutual respect and admiration for each other's unique contribution to the whole, which leads to loving relationships in which each half of the whole can flourish.

Supporters of the more biblically consistent complementarianism view are increasingly finding themselves attacked by those who throw out terms such as "misogyny," which is the hatred of women. Much of contemporary egalitarianism emerges from a secular worldview that not only pits men against women but is opposed to hierarchical relationships that are part of God's created order. In God's world order, Adam came first, and from his flesh, God created Eve (1 Corinthians 11:8–11).[40]

Embodied in this understanding of the created order is "primogeniture," the concept that attaches significance to being born first. This pertains to Adam being formed first, with the rights of the firstborn when it comes to inheritance and rights of succession. Primogeniture is a difficult concept in our society today, but it is important for us to maintain a scriptural understanding of men and women. This goes back to 1 Timothy 2:13, where Paul states, "Adam was formed first, then Eve." Adam's position as first-created person places him in a more senior role in the creation order and lends credence to the arguments of his headship.

An honest reading of the Bible finds this view of male headship and authority reflected by the authors of the Bible throughout the canon of Scripture. Even so, these concepts are focused on the home and the church. While the Bible speaks a lot about husbands and wives and the place of women in church leadership, I do not believe this supports the view that men have authority over every woman they encounter in workplace or church settings.

CONCLUDING OBSERVATIONS

WHEN WE LOOK IN the Bible, we find men and women being used of God in accordance with their spiritual gifts and according to complementarity. Even in the Old Testament, an era in which women had fewer rights than they did during the time of Jesus, we find women in leadership roles according to their positioning and callings. Let us be careful to note that God used Deborah as a judge and a prophetess who led an army when none of the men were brave enough to lead (Judges 4–5). And in the New Testament, Phoebe is believed to have been a deaconess; Lydia was a wealthy business owner and church leader who opened her home to others; and Priscilla and her husband, Aquila, were a ministry team. We should not place limits on God when it comes to how he might want to use women in the church.

This means women can be used equally with men in areas where their professional training and spiritual gifts give them special knowledge and insights. Elders and lead ministers submitted to the Holy Spirit should seek the Lord on a regular basis to identify those placed in the body to further the kingdom of God regardless of whether they are male or female.

One last observation: church leaders need to recognize that single women in their congregation might experience the church differently than married couples or even single men. Single women might find fewer opportunities to socialize or participate in events designed to accommodate married couples. Single women may also find themselves more vulnerable to unwanted sexual advances.

Church leaders seeking to avoid problems must exercise wisdom and prudence. Every church needs to have clear lines of communication and safe channels where abuses of authority and dangerous practices can be detected and addressed. This must be done *before* churches find themselves in situations of an accusation, which can lead to the breakdown of trust and the disintegration of the church body.

REFLECTION & DISCUSSION QUESTIONS

1. Read John 4:1–42. How does this story display Jesus' view of women?

_____

_____

_____

_____

_____

_____

2. What does Genesis 1:26–28 imply about God's design regarding male and female?

_____

_____

_____

_____

_____

_____

3. Discuss the difference between complementarianism and egalitarianism. What has been your personal position on this issue?

_____

_____

_____

_____

_____

_____

4. How have societal and professional roles, as well as the breakdown of traditional marriage, impacted your views on male headship in the family? How has it affected your view of those with whom you are in relationship?

_____

_____

_____

_____

_____

_____

5. Read Ephesians 5:25. Practically, what would it look like for a husband to love his wife "as Christ loved the church and gave himself up for her"?

6. Is this teaching on male leadership in the home and church challenging for you? If so, pray for wisdom and for God to clarify his Word and open your eyes to examples of his will in this area.

5

HOW SHOULD WE VIEW MATERIALISM?

Answer: Materialism is sin because it causes us to focus on the acquisition of earthly treasures and rewards that detract from spiritual blessings and riches that come from being in a right relationship with Jesus.

Do not love the world or anything in
the world. If anyone loves the world,
love for the Father is not in them.
— 1 John 2:15

Malcolm Forbes, one of the world's wealthiest men at the time of his death, is said to have coined the phrase, "He who dies with the most toys wins."[41] Although Forbes's wealth allowed him to travel and amass many toys and luxuries, his mindset about life and enjoying the pleasures that money could buy contradicts the teaching found in Matthew 6:19–21, where Jesus tells us:

> Do not store up for yourselves treasures on earth, where moths and vermin destroy, and where thieves break in and steal. But store up for yourselves treasures in heaven, where moths and vermin do not destroy, and where thieves do not break in and steal. For where your treasure is, there your heart will be also.

Forbes lived through the Great Depression and was a member of the Greatest Generation, a demographic comprising people born between 1901 and 1927. This generation also endured the New Deal, two World Wars, and the turmoil of the 1960s. When Forbes died in 1990, he was remembered for his extravagant lifestyle and his interests in capitalism and free markets, but what about his treasures in the kingdom?

Proverbs 22:1 tells us, "A good name is more desirable than great riches; to be esteemed is better than silver or gold." What we learn from this Scripture is that the value of having a good name while on earth is worth more than acquiring wealth on earth. In other words, Forbes's priorities weren't straight, and he didn't win at the most important aspects of life, according to the Bible. A person's character is the true measure of wealth, and it largely determines the impact they have on others

A PERSON'S CHARACTER IS THE TRUE MEASURE OF WEALTH.

who watch them walk through life, whether they be family members or others God places in their paths. A poor man with integrity is richer than a deceiver or a corrupt man (Proverbs 19:1; 28:6).

CHOOSING BETWEEN GRATITUDE AND GREED

While previous chapters in this book have dealt with our relationships with our fellow humans, it is important to recognize that our calling to countercultural living also extends to our relationship with the material world. A greedy disposition toward the material world has led to many significant problems, such as theft, warfare, betrayal, and waste. When we are on our death beds, we can minimize our regrets by learning from God what is truly important while we have an opportunity to make lasting differences in the lives of those who look to us for leadership and guidance.

The *Cambridge Dictionary* defines materialism as "the belief that having money, possessions, and comfort are the most important things in life."[42] We can become preoccupied with money to the point of greed. And greed manifests itself as an insatiable desire for more of whatever we lust after, whether it be money, possessions, or rewards. A greedy person never has enough. They are reluctant to share, and such behavior can lead to hoarding. The Old and New Testaments have a lot to teach us about the subject of money, greed, and hoarding. 1 Timothy 6:10 warns that "the love of money is a root of all kinds of evil. Some people, eager for money, have wandered from the faith and pierced themselves with many griefs." Continuing this theme, Paul states in 1 Timothy 6:17–19:

> Command those who are rich in this present world not to be arrogant nor to put their hope in wealth, which is so uncertain, but to put their hope in God, who richly provides us with everything for our enjoyment. Command them to do good, to be rich in good deeds, and to be generous and willing to share. In this way they will lay up treasure for themselves as a firm foundation for the coming

age, so that they may take hold of the life that is truly life.

Showing us how greed operates, Ecclesiastes 5:10 warns, "Whoever loves money never has enough; whoever loves wealth is never satisfied with their income. This too is meaningless."

One of the most sobering examples of greed and short-sightedness is found in Jesus' interactions with a man that ended with the parable of the rich fool (Luke 12:13–21). A man approached Jesus to complain about his brother's failure to divide the family inheritance with him. In the ancient world, it was not unusual for the firstborn son to inherit a double portion of the inheritance. How and whether he shared with others might have been a personal choice. Before Jesus told the parable, he pointed out to the man that he was not appointed as judge to this family matter. He warned the brother to watch out for greed because life is about much more than possessions.

To illustrate his point, Jesus delivered a parable about a rich man who had been blessed with an abundance of crops (Luke 12:16–21). Noticing that he had no place to store the harvest, he decided, "This is what I'll do. I will tear down my barns and build bigger ones, and there I will store my surplus grain. And I'll say to myself, 'You have plenty of grain laid up for many years. Take life easy;

eat, drink and be merry'" (vv. 18–19). The story continues: "But God said to him, 'You fool! This very night your life will be demanded from you. Then who will get what you have prepared for yourself?' This is how it will be with whoever stores up things for themselves but is not rich toward God (vv. 20–21)."

Certainly, Jesus' parable was not the interaction this man was expecting, but it offered to him and to us a valuable reminder about what is enormously important in life, and just how little we fragile human beings can control. We cannot control the length of our days or the manner of our deaths unless we foolishly take our own lives. We can amass riches and possessions, but when we leave this earth, we also leave behind our possessions for someone else to enjoy or to squander. Estate planning is all we can really control. As 1 Peter 1:24 reminds us, "All flesh is like grass and all its glory like the flower of grass. The grass withers, and the flower falls" (ESV). And in Hebrews 13:5 God offers himself to us and tells us to be content with what we have because he will never leave us nor forsake us.

> **WE CANNOT CONTROL THE LENGTH OF OUR DAYS.**

FAME AND FORTUNE

WE ALL HAVE OUR favorite sins. I do not think of myself as a greedy person, obsessed with the desire to acquire material possessions or to amass wealth just for the sake of getting wealthy. But one sin and temptation I *have* wrestled with has to do with seeking recognition for my work and accomplishments. Still, I often experience disappointment when I feel that I have been slighted or passed over for an award that I felt certain I deserved. And we're all tempted to make excuses for ourselves. My excuse for wanting recognition and credit for accomplishments could be connected with my status as a racial minority or the poverty that shaped my early life. I experienced much rejection in my life. But by the grace of God, I worked hard and became a tenured professor at Princeton and later Vanderbilt. It was there that I first earned national awards and recognition, often while experiencing a palpable depression and sense of emptiness that persisted even after I received the early tenure that I had made an obsession. Tenure, national awards, and accolades did not bring me the satisfaction and happiness I thought would ensue.

In fact, the accomplishment of my goals is what threw me into a deep depression. What followed was a spiritual journey that culminated with my Christian conversion experience, where for the first time in my life I understood the gospel message and received the freedom that comes from a relationship with Christ. Only through Christ did I find my peace and a sense of well-being that comes from understanding who I am in Christ and how he is working in my life. God saved me and freed me from a crippling shyness that had limited my ability to communicate in front of audiences. By his grace, I now have opportunities to speak in forums that reach millions.

Like anyone else, I sometimes fall into a dangerous trap when I get too focused on myself and the accolades people shower upon me. Perhaps this is one reason why success can lead to a person's downfall. That is, if they begin to take themselves too seriously and forget the role God played in choosing and blessing them. According to John 12:43, we can find ourselves in a fallen state, where we value the praise of men more than our love of God. This passage puts everything in good perspective.

> Do not love the world or the things in the world. If anyone loves the world, the love of the Father is not in him. For all that is in the world—the desires of the flesh and the desires of the eyes and pride of life—is not from the Father but is from the world. (1 John 2:15–16, ESV)

Our protection from the traps of materialism, greed, and the quest for fame and fortune come from our relationship with Christ. God wants us to walk under the guidance of the Holy Spirit and not to succumb to the desires of the flesh that will always be nearby to tempt us. If we stay rightly connected with Christ, his people, and his Word, we have supernatural strength to resist the works of the flesh that inevitably lead to our downfall if we do not resist them (Galatians 5:16–26).

MONEY AND STEWARDSHIP

So WHAT IS THE alternative to materialism? Stewardship. God expects us to be good stewards of the money and wealth and prosperity that he pours out on his people. Much wisdom about wealth is found in Proverbs where saving money and hard work are associated with wisdom (Proverbs 21:20; 14:23). We are warned about get-rich schemes and about boasting about our riches (Proverbs 28:20, 22; Jeremiah 9:23–24). As Christians, we are to be generous with our wealth (2 Corinthians 9:6; Luke 6:38; Acts 20:35), cheerful when we give (2 Corinthians 9:7), content with what we have (Philippians 4:11), and generous when it comes to meeting the needs of others (Matthew 25:35–40). We are also called to support the work of the church and to do so cheerfully.

In the various ways our Christian values are tested and tried, let us always remember that we are Jesus' disciples and discipleship has a cost (Luke 14:28–33).

REFLECTION & DISCUSSION QUESTIONS

1. Did you grow up materially poor, comfortable, or wealthy by US standards? How has the way you grew up impacted your view of money today?

2. Have you discussed materialism in your home? If you've discussed it, have you defined it clearly and called it sin?

3. Give examples of how our society values financial success over good character.

_____

_____

_____

_____

_____

_____

4. Read 1 Timothy 6:17–19. What are specific ways that you can protect yourself from becoming too preoccupied with money and possessions?

_____

_____

_____

_____

_____

_____

5. How can we be wise financially without becoming greedy and selfish?

_____

_____

_____

_____

_____

_____

6. According to this chapter, "We are Jesus' disciples and discipleship has a cost." What are some ways that being a disciple of Jesus has cost you? What are some ways that you think it should cost you?

_____

_____

_____

_____

_____

_____

_____

APPENDIX A

BOOK RECOMMENDATIONS FOR FURTHER STUDY

Bobby Harrington, Renee Sproles, Daniel McCoy, Rick Oster, et al., "On Gender and the Bible," a twelve-part series at Renew.org, https://renew.org/on-gender-and-the-bible-a-summary-part-12/.

Carol M. Swain and Christopher J. Schorr, *Black Eye for America: How Critical Race Theory Is Burning Down the House* (Nashville: Be the People Publications, 2021).

Carol M. Swain, *Be the People: A Call to Reclaim America's Faith and Promise* (Nashville: Thomas Nelson, 2011).

Helen Pluckrose and James Lindsay, *Cynical Theories: How Activist Scholarship Made Everything About Race* (Durham: Pitchstone Publishing, 2020).

Steve Feazel and Carol M. Swain, *Abduction: How Liberalism Steals Our Children's Hearts and Minds* (Meadville: Christian Faith Publishing, 2016).

Thaddeus J. Williams, *Confronting Injustice Without Compromising Truth* (Grand Rapids: Zondervan, 2020).

APPENDIX B

Mission: We Renew the Teachings of Jesus to Fuel Disciple Making

Vision: A collaborative network equipping millions of disciples, disciple makers, and church planters among all ethnicities.

SEVEN VALUES

RENEWAL IN THE BIBLE and in history follows a discernible outline that can be summarized by seven key elements. We champion these elements as our core values.

They are listed in a sequential pattern that is typical of renewal, and it all starts with God.

1. *Renewing by God's Spirit.* We believe that God is the author of renewal and that he invites us to access and join him through prayer and fasting for the Holy Spirit's work of renewal.
2. *Following God's Word.* We learn the ways of God with lasting clarity and conviction by trusting God's Word and what it teaches as the objective foundation for renewal and life.
3. *Surrendering to Jesus' Lordship.* The gospel teaches us that Jesus is Messiah (King) and Lord. He calls everyone to salvation (in eternity) and discipleship (in this life) through a faith commitment that is expressed in repentance, confession, and baptism. Repentance and surrender to Jesus as Lord is the never-ending cycle for life in Jesus' kingdom, and it is empowered by the Spirit.
4. *Championing disciple making.* Jesus personally gave us his model of disciple making, which he demonstrated with his disciples. Those same principles from the life of Jesus should be utilized as we make disciples today and champion discipleship as the core mission of the local church.
5. *Loving like Jesus.* Jesus showed us the true meaning of love and taught us that sacrificial love is the

distinguishing character trait of true disciples (and true renewal). Sacrificial love is the foundation for our relationships both in the church and in the world.

6. *Living in holiness.* Just as Jesus lived differently from the world, the people in his church will learn to live differently than the world. Even when it is difficult, we show that God's kingdom is an alternative kingdom to the world.

7. *Leading courageously.* God always uses leaders in renewal who live by a prayerful, risk-taking faith. Renewal will be led by bold and courageous leaders—who make disciples, plant churches, and create disciple making movements.

TEN FAITH STATEMENTS

WE BELIEVE THAT JESUS Christ is Lord. We are a group of church leaders inviting others to join the theological and disciple making journey described below. We want to trust and follow Jesus Christ to the glory of God the Father in the power of the Holy Spirit. We are committed to *restoring* the kingdom vision of Jesus and the apostles, especially the *message* of Jesus' gospel, the *method* of disciple making he showed us, and the *model* of what a community of his disciples, at their best, can become.

We live in a time when cultural pressures are forcing us to face numerous difficulties and complexities in following God. Many are losing their resolve. We trust that God is gracious and forgives the errors of those with genuine faith in his Son, but our desire is to be faithful in all things.

Our focus is disciple making, which is both reaching lost people (evangelism) and bringing people to maturity (sanctification). We seek to be a movement of disciple making leaders who make disciples and other disciple makers. We want to renew existing churches and help plant multiplying churches.

1. *God's Word.* We believe God gave us the sixty-six books of the Bible to be received as the inspired, authoritative, and infallible Word of God for salvation and life. The documents of Scripture come to us as diverse literary and historical writings. Despite their complexities, they can be understood, trusted, and followed. We want to do the hard work of wrestling to understand Scripture in order to obey God. We want to avoid the errors of interpreting Scripture through the sentimental lens of our feelings and opinions or through a complex re-interpretation of plain meanings so that the Bible says what our culture says. Ours is a time for both clear thinking and courage. Because the Holy Spirit inspired all sixty-six books, we honor Jesus' Lordship by submitting our lives to all that God has for us in them.

Psalm 1; 119; Deuteronomy 4:1–6; 6:1–9;
2 Chronicles 34; Nehemiah 8; Matthew 5:1–7:28;
15:6–9; John 12:44–50; Matthew 28:19; Acts 2:42;
17:10–11; 2 Timothy 3:16–4:4; 1 Peter 1:20–21.

2. *Christian convictions.* We believe the Scriptures reveal three distinct elements of the faith: *essential* elements which are necessary for salvation; *important* elements which are to be pursued so that we faithfully follow Christ; and *personal* elements or opinion. The gospel is *essential.* Every person who is indwelt and sealed by God's Holy Spirit because of their faith in the gospel is a brother or a sister in Christ. *Important* but secondary elements of the faith are vital. Our faithfulness to God requires us to seek and pursue them, even as we acknowledge that our salvation may not be dependent on getting them right. And thirdly, there are personal matters of opinion, disputable areas where God gives us personal freedom. But we are never at liberty to express our freedom in a way that causes others to stumble in sin. In all things, we want to show understanding, kindness, and love.

1 Corinthians 15:1–8; Romans 1:15–17;
Galatians 1:6–9; 2 Timothy 2:8; Ephesians 1:13–14;
4:4–6; Romans 8:9; 1 Corinthians 12:13;
1 Timothy 4:16; 2 Timothy 3:16–4:4;

> *Matthew 15:6–9; Acts 20:32; 1 Corinthians 11:1–2;*
> *1 John 2:3–4; 2 Peter 3:14–16; Romans 14:1–23.*

3. *The gospel.* We believe God created all things and made human beings in his image, so that we could enjoy a relationship with him and each other. But we lost our way, through Satan's influence. We are now spiritually dead, separated from God. Without his help, we gravitate toward sin and self-rule. The gospel is God's good news of reconciliation. It was promised to Abraham and David and revealed in Jesus' life, ministry, teaching, and sacrificial death on the cross. The gospel is the saving action of the triune God. The Father sent the Son into the world to take on human flesh and redeem us. Jesus came as the promised Messiah of the Old Testament. He ushered in the kingdom of God, died for our sins according to Scripture, was buried, and was raised on the third day. He defeated sin and death and ascended to heaven. He is seated at the right hand of God as Lord and he is coming back for his disciples. Through the Spirit, we are transformed and sanctified. God will raise everyone for the final judgment. Those who trusted and followed Jesus by faith will not experience punishment for their sins and separation from God in hell. Instead, we will join together with God in the renewal of all things in the consummated kingdom. We will live together in

the new heaven and new earth where we will glorify God and enjoy him forever.

> *Genesis 1–3; Romans 3:10–12; 7:8–25;*
> *Genesis 12:1–3; Galatians 3:6–9; Isaiah 11:1–4;*
> *2 Samuel 7:1–16; Micah 5:2–4; Daniel 2:44–45;*
> *Luke 1:33; John 1:1–3; Matthew 4:17;*
> *1 Corinthians 15:1–8; Acts 1:11; 2:36; 3:19–21;*
> *Colossians 3:1; Matthew 25:31–32; Revelation 21:1ff;*
> *Romans 3:21–26.*

4. *Faithful faith.* We believe that people are saved by grace through faith. The gospel of Jesus' kingdom calls people to both salvation and discipleship—no exceptions, no excuses. Faith is more than mere intellectual agreement or emotional warmth toward God. It is living and active; faith is surrendering our self-rule to the rule of God through Jesus in the power of the Spirit. We surrender by trusting and following Jesus as both Savior and Lord in all things. Faith includes allegiance, loyalty, and faithfulness to him.

> *Ephesians 2:8–9; Mark 8:34–38; Luke 14:25–35;*
> *Romans 1:3, 5; 16:25–26; Galatians 2:20;*
> *James 2:14–26; Matthew 7:21–23; Galatians 4:19;*
> *Matthew 28:19–20; 2 Corinthians 3:3, 17–18;*
> *Colossians 1:28.*

5. *New birth*. God so loved the world that he gave his one and only Son, that whoever believes in him shall not perish but have eternal life. To believe in Jesus means we trust and follow him as both Savior and Lord. When we commit to trust and follow Jesus, we express this faith by repenting from sin, confessing his name, and receiving baptism by immersion in water. Baptism, as an expression of faith, is for the remission of sins. We uphold baptism as the normative means of entry into the life of discipleship. It marks our commitment to regularly die to ourselves and rise to live for Christ in the power of the Holy Spirit. We believe God sovereignly saves as he sees fit, but we are bound by Scripture to uphold this teaching about surrendering to Jesus in faith through repentance, confession, and baptism.

> *1 Corinthians 8:6; John 3:1–9; 3:16–18;*
> *3:19–21; Luke 13:3–5; 24:46–47; Acts 2:38;*
> *3:19; 8:36–38; 16:31–33; 17:30; 20:21; 22:16;*
> *26:20; Galatians 3:26–27; Romans 6:1–4;*
> *10:9–10; 1 Peter 3:21; Romans 2:25–29;*
> *2 Chronicles 30:17–19; Matthew 28:19–20;*
> *Galatians 2:20; Acts 18:24–26.*

6. *Holy Spirit*. We believe God's desire is for everyone to be saved and come to the knowledge of the truth. Many hear the gospel but do not believe it because they

are blinded by Satan and resist the pull of the Holy Spirit. We encourage everyone to listen to the Word and let the Holy Spirit convict them of their sin and draw them into a relationship with God through Jesus. We believe that when we are born again and indwelt by the Holy Spirit, we are to live as people who are filled, empowered, and led by the Holy Spirit. This is how we walk with God and discern his voice. A prayerful life, rich in the Holy Spirit, is fundamental to true discipleship and living in step with the kingdom reign of Jesus. We seek to be a prayerful, Spirit-led fellowship.

> *1 Timothy 2:4; John 16:7–11; Acts 7:51;*
> *1 John 2:20, 27; John 3:5; Ephesians 1:13–14;*
> *5:18; Galatians 5:16–25; Romans 8:5–11;*
> *Acts 1:14; 2:42; 6:6; 9:40; 12:5; 13:3; 14:23; 20:36;*
> *2 Corinthians 3:3.*

7. *Disciple making.* We believe the core mission of the local church is making disciples of Jesus Christ—it is God's plan "A" to redeem the world and manifest the reign of his kingdom. We want to be disciples who make disciples because of our love for God and others. We personally seek to become more and more like Jesus through his Spirit so that Jesus would live through us. To help us focus on Jesus, his sacrifice on the cross, our unity in him, and his coming return, we typically share communion

in our weekly gatherings. We desire the fruits of biblical disciple making which are disciples who live and love like Jesus and "go" into every corner of society and to the ends of the earth. Disciple making is the engine that drives our missional service to those outside the church. We seek to be known where we live for the good that we do in our communities. We love and serve all people, as Jesus did, no strings attached. At the same time, as we do good for others, we also seek to form relational bridges that we prayerfully hope will open doors for teaching people the gospel of the kingdom and the way of salvation.

> *Matthew 28:19–20; Galatians 4:19;*
> *Acts 2:41; Philippians 1:20–21; Colossians 1:27–29;*
> *2 Corinthians 3:3; 1 Thessalonians 2:19–20;*
> *John 13:34–35; 1 John 3:16; 1 Corinthians 13:1–13;*
> *Luke 22:14–23; 1 Corinthians 11:17–24; Acts 20:7.*

8. *Kingdom life.* We believe in the present kingdom reign of God, the power of the Holy Spirit to transform people, and the priority of the local church. God's holiness should lead our churches to reject lifestyles characterized by pride, sexual immorality, homosexuality, easy divorce, idolatry, greed, materialism, gossip, slander, racism, violence, and the like. God's love should lead our churches to emphasize love as the distinguishing sign of a true disciple. Love for one another should make the church

like an extended family—a fellowship of married people, singles, elderly, and children who are all brothers and sisters to one another. The love of the extended church family to one another is vitally important. Love should be expressed in both service to the church and to the surrounding community. It leads to the breaking down of walls (racial, social, political), evangelism, acts of mercy, compassion, forgiveness, and the like. By demonstrating the ways of Jesus, the church reveals God's kingdom reign to the watching world.

> *1 Corinthians 1:2; Galatians 5:19–21;*
> *Ephesians 5:3–7; Colossians 3:5–9;*
> *Matthew 19:3–12; Romans 1:26–32; 14:17–18;*
> *1 Peter 1:15–16; Matthew 25:31–46;*
> *John 13:34–35; Colossians 3:12–13; 1 John 3:16;*
> *1 Corinthians 13:1–13; 2 Corinthians 5:16–21.*

9. *Counter-cultural living.* We believe Jesus' Lordship through Scripture will lead us to be a distinct light in the world. We follow the first and second Great Commandments where love and loyalty to God come first and love for others comes second. So we prioritize the gospel and one's relationship with God, with a strong commitment to love people in their secondary points of need too. The gospel is God's light for us. It teaches us grace, mercy, and love. It also teaches us God's holiness,

justice, and the reality of hell which led to Jesus' sacrifice of atonement for us. God's light is grace and truth, mercy and righteousness, love and holiness. God's light among us should be reflected in distinctive ways like the following:

A. We believe that human life begins at conception and ends upon natural death, and that all human life is priceless in the eyes of God. All humans should be treated as image-bearers of God. For this reason, we stand for the sanctity of life both at its beginning and its end. We oppose elective abortions and euthanasia as immoral and sinful. We understand that there are very rare circumstances that may lead to difficult choices when a mother or child's life is at stake, and we prayerfully surrender and defer to God's wisdom, grace, and mercy in those circumstances.

B. We believe God created marriage as the context for the expression and enjoyment of sexual relations. Jesus defines marriage as a covenant between one man and one woman. We believe that all sexual activity outside the bounds of marriage, including same-sex unions and same-sex marriage, are immoral and must not be condoned by disciples of Jesus.

C. We believe that Jesus invites all races and ethnicities into the kingdom of God. Because humanity has exhibited grave racial injustices throughout history, we believe that everyone, especially disciples, must be proactive in securing justice for people of all races and that racial reconciliation must be a priority for the church.

D. We believe that both men and women were created by God to equally reflect, in gendered ways, the nature and character of God in the world. In marriage, husbands and wives are to submit to one another, yet there are gender specific expressions: husbands model themselves in relationship with their wives after Jesus' sacrificial love for the church, and wives model themselves in relationship with their husbands after the church's willingness to follow Jesus. In the church, men and women serve as partners in the use of their gifts in ministry, while seeking to uphold New Testament norms which teach that the lead teacher/preacher role in the gathered church and the elder/overseer role are for qualified men. The vision of the Bible is an equal partnership of men and women in creation, in marriage, in salvation, in the gifts of the Spirit, and in the ministries of the church but exercised in ways that honor gender as described in the Bible.

E. We believe that we must resist the forces of culture that focus on materialism and greed. The Bible teaches that the love of money is the root of all sorts of evil and that greed is idolatry. Disciples of Jesus should joyfully give liberally and work sacrificially for the poor, the marginalized, and the oppressed.

> *Romans 12:3–8; Matthew 22:36–40; 1 Corinthians 12:4–7; Ephesians 2:10; 4:11–13; 1 Peter 4:10–11; Matthew 20:24–27; Philippians 1:1; Acts 20:28; 1 Timothy 2:11–15; 3:1–7; Titus 1:5–9; 1 Corinthians 11:2–9; 14:33–36; Ephesians 5:21–33; Colossians 3:18–19; 1 Corinthians 7:32–35.*

10. *The end.* We believe that Jesus is coming back to earth in order to bring this age to an end. Jesus will reward the saved and punish the wicked, and finally destroy God's last enemy, death. He will put all things under the Father, so that God may be all in all forever. That is why we have urgency for the Great Commission— to make disciples of all nations. We like to look at the Great Commission as an inherent part of God's original command to "be fruitful and multiply." We want to be

disciples of Jesus who love people and help them to be disciples of Jesus. We are a movement of disciples who make disciples who help renew existing churches and who start new churches that make more disciples. We want to reach as many as possible—until Jesus returns and God restores all creation to himself in the new heaven and new earth.

Matthew 25:31–32; Acts 17:31; Revelation 20:11–15; 2 Thessalonians 1:6–10; Mark 9:43–49; Luke 12:4–7; Acts 4:12; John 14:6; Luke 24:46–48; Matthew 28:19–20; Genesis 12:1–3; Galatians 2:20; 4:19; Luke 6:40; Luke 19:10; Revelation 21:1ff.

NOTES

1. "In U.S. Decline of Christianity Continues at a Rapid Pace," PewForum, October 17, 2019, https://www.pewforum.org/2019/10/17/in-u-s-decline-of-christianity-continues-at-rapid-pace/.

2. (San Francisco: Encounter Books, 2004).

3. "Shout Your Abortion," accessed May 24, 2021, https://shoutyourabortion.com/.

4. Henry T. Greely, "Human Reproductive Cloning: The Curious Incident of the Dog in the Night-Time," February 21, 2020, https://www.statnews.com/2020/02/21/human-reproductive-cloning-curious-incident-of-the-dog-in-the-night-time/.

5. Aparna Vidyasagar, "Human-Animal Chimeras: Biological Research & Ethical Issues," September 29, 2016, https://www.livescience.com/56309-human-animal-chimeras.html.

6. Gary Sutanto, "Herman Bavinck and the Image of God," September 1, 2020, accessed May 24, 20201, https://www.pastortheologians.com/articles/2020/9/1/

humanity-in-its-entirety-herman-bavinck-and-the-im-age-of-god.

7. Medina Estévez, *Male and Female He Created Them: On Marriage and the Family* (San Francisco: Ignatius, 2003), 19–20.

8. C. S. Lewis, *Mere Christianity* (New York: Macmillan, 1952), 102.

9. For more information, see Renee Sproles and Rick Oster, "On Gender and the Bible: What About Husbands and Wives?" Renew.org, May 24, 2021, https://renew.org/on-gender-and-the-bible-what-about-husbands-and-wives-part-6/.

10. W. Bradford Wilcox and Steven L. Nock, "What's Love Got to Do with It? Equality, Equity, Commitment, and Women's Marital Quality," *Social Forces* vol. 84, no. 3 (March 2006): 1339.

11. Maggie Gallagher, *The Abolition of Marriage* (Washington, DC: Regnery, 1996), 9.

12. W. Bradford Wilcox, *Soft Patriarchs, New Men: How Christianity Shapes Fathers and Husbands* (Chicago: University of Chicago Press, 2004).

13. W. Bradford Wilcox, "Religion and the Domestication of Men," *Contexts* (Fall 2006): 42.

14. Ibid., 44. See also W. Bradford Wilcox and Nicholas Wolfinger, "Living and Loving 'Decent': Religion and Relationship Quality Among Urban Parents," *Social Science Research* 37 (2008): 828–843. For

a contrary view, Joe Carter, "Why Complementarian Men Do More Housework," January 11, 2021, https://www.thegospelcoalition.org/article/why-complementarian-men-do-more-housework/.

15. For more information, see Kevin DeYoung, *What Does the Bible Really Teach About Homosexuality?* (Crossway, 2015).

16. Philip S. Foner, *History of Black Americans: From Africa to the Emergence of the Cotton Kingdom* (Westport: Greenwood, 1975), 191.

17. Joe R. Feagin and Clairece Feagin, *Racial and Ethnic Relations*, 6th ed. (Upper Saddle River, NJ: Prentice Hall, 1999), 6.

18. Arthur Schlesinger, Jr., *The Disuniting of America* (Knoxville: Whittle Direct Books, 1991), 48.

19. David Goldenberg, "The Curse of Ham, Race and Slavery in Early Judaism," (Princeton, NJ: Princeton University, 2003), https://www.researchgate.net/publication/263161577_The_Curse_of_Ham_Race_and_Slavery_in_Early_Judaism_Christianity_and_Islam.

20. This list is quoted from Daniel McCoy, "Corrupted or Co-opted: 2 Non-Options as Christians Fight Racism," Renew.org, https://renew.org/corrupted-or-co-opted-2-non-options-as-christians-fight-racism/.

21. For example, see Pastor Ronnie Floyd, as quoted in Abigail Robertson, "'A Divided Church Cannot Call a Divided Nation to Unity': Hundreds Pray in US Capitol

on National Day of Prayer," CBS News, May 4, 2018, https://www1.cbn.com/cbnnews/politics/2018/may/a-divided-church-cannot-call-a-divided-nation-to-unity-hundreds-pray-in-us-capitol-on-national-day-of-prayer.

22. Neil Shenvi, "Social Justice, Critical Theory, and Christianity: Are They Compatible?" Southeastern Baptist Theological Seminary, April 29, 2020, YouTube video, 57:14, https://www.youtube.com/watch?v=E33aunwGQQ4.

23. Gerry McDermott, "Critical Race Theory: Is It Compatible with the Christian Faith?" February 10, 2020, https://www.patheos.com/blogs/northamptonseminar/2020/02/10/critical-race-theory-iii-is-it-compatible-with-christian-faith/; Gerry McDermott, ed., *Race and Covenant: Recovering the Religious Roots for American Reconciliation* (Grand Rapids: Acton Institute, 2020).

24. Neil Shenvi and Pat Sawyer, "The Incompatibility of Critical Theory and Christianity," *The Gospel Coalition*, May 15, 2019, https://www.thegospelcoalition.org/article/incompatibility-critical-theory-christianity/.

25. Robin DeAngelo, *White Fragility: Why It's So Hard for White People to Talk About Racism* (Boston: Beacon Press, 2018).

26. Gerry McDermott, and Thaddeus J. Williams, *Confronting Injustice Without Compromising Truth* (Grand Rapids: Zondervan, 2020).

27. David W. Swanson, *Rediscipling the White Church: From Cheap Diversity to True Solidarity* (Downers Grove, IL: InterVarsity Press, 2020); Daniel Hill, *White Awake: An Honest Look at What It Means to Be White* (Downers Grove, IL: Intervarsity Press, 2017).

28. Alisa Childers, *Another Gospel: A Lifelong Christian Seeks Truth in Response to Progressive Christianity* (Carol Stream, IL: Tyndale Momentum, 2020).

29. See "The #MeToo Movement and the Law," *FindLaw*, November 13, 2018, accessed January 22, 2021, https://www.findlaw.com/employment/employment-discrimination/the--metoo-movement-and-the-law.html, and "Sexual Abuse Cases in Churches," *Newsome/Melton*, October 23, 2020, accessed January 22, 2021, https://www.newsomelaw.com/blog/sexual-abuse-cases-in-churches/.

30. John Money, J. J. Hampson and Hampson J. L., "An Examination of Some Basic Sexual Concepts: The Evidence of Human Hermaphroditism," *Bull Johns Hopkins Hospital* 97, no. 4 (October 1955): 301–19.

31. Carol Chetkovich, "How Non-Binary Gender Definitions Confound (Already Complex) Thinking About Gender and Public Policy," *Journal of Public Affairs Education* vol. 25, no. 2 (2019): 226–252, https://www.tandfonline.com/doi/full/10.1080/15236803.2018.1565050.

32. *Open Education Sociology Dictionary*, accessed January 22, 2021, https://sociologydictionary.org/gender/#definition_of_gender.

33. See Darren Williamson and Ellen Radcliff, "On Gender and the Bible: Thoughts of a Theologian and a Therapist on the Transgender Debate," Renew.org, accessed June 23, 2021, https://renew.org/on-gender-and-the-bible-thoughts-of-a-theologian-and-a-therapist-on-the-transgender-debate-part-11/.

34. See helpful guidelines promoted by the Assemblies of God, http://religiousinstitute.org/denom_statements/transgenderism-transsexuality-gender-identity/.

35. "Complementarianism," *Theopedia*, accessed January 24, 2021, https://www.theopedia.com/complementarianism.

36. Alyssa Roat, "What Are Complementarianism and Egalitarianism? What's the Difference?" accessed January 20, 2021, https://www.christianity.com/wiki/christian-terms/what-are-complementarianism-and-egalitarianism-what-s-the-difference.html.

37. See the summary article by Bobby Harrington and Renee Sproles, "On Gender and the Bible: A Summary (Part 12)" https://renew.org/on-gender-and-the-bible-a-summary-part-12/.

38. Robert W. Yarbrough, *The Letters to Timothy and Titus* (Grand Rapids: Eerdmans, 2018), 140–182; ed. Andreas Kostenberger, Thomas Schreiner, and Denny

Burk, *Women in the Church: An Interpretation and Application of 1 Timothy 2:1–15* (CrossWay Books, 2016).

39. For more on this topic, see the twelve-part series titled, "On Gender and the Bible" led by Bobby Harrington, Renee Sproles, and Daniel McCoy at Renew.org, https://renew.org/on-gender-and-the-bible-a-summary-part-12/.

40. Bobby Harrington and Renee Sproles, "On Gender and the Bible: Where Does Egalitarianism Lead? (Part 9)," Renew.org, accessed May 24, 2021, https://renew.org/on-gender-and-the-bible-where-does-egalitarianism-lead-part-9/.

41. Robert Forbes, "My Father, Malcolm Forbes: a Never-Ending Adventure," *Forbes*, August 19, 2021, https://www.forbes.com/sites/forbesdigitalcovers/2019/08/19/my-father-malcolm-forbes-a-never-ending-adventure/?sh=65a10f119fbb.

42. *Cambridge Dictionary*, s.v. "materialism," accessed June 18, 2021, https://dictionary.cambridge.org/us/dictionary/english/materialism.

Made in the USA
Coppell, TX
01 August 2022

80757834R00079